# It's another Quality Book from CGP

This book is for anyone doing Edexcel Modular GCSE Mathematics
at Intermediate Level.

Whatever subject you're doing it's the same
old story — there are lots of facts and you've just got
to learn them.  KS4 Maths is no different.

Happily this CGP book gives you all that important
information as clearly and concisely as possible.

It's also got some daft bits in to try and make the whole
experience at least vaguely entertaining for you.

# What CGP is all about

Our sole aim here at CGP is to produce the highest quality
books — carefully written, immaculately presented and
dangerously close to being funny.

Then we work our socks off to get them out to you
— at the cheapest possible prices.

# Contents

Published by Coordination Group Publications Ltd.
Written by Richard Parsons
Design Editor: Ruso Bradley
Updated by: Philippa Falshaw, Tim Major, Julie Schofield

ISBN 1 84146 003 6
Groovy website: www.cgpbooks.co.uk
With thanks to Rosemary Cartwright for the proofreading.
Printed by Elanders Hindson, Newcastle upon Tyne.

# Big Numbers & Rounding Off

## Putting Numbers in Order of Size

<u>Example</u>:  12   84   623   32   486   4,563   75   2,143

① It may not be exactly difficult, but it's still best to do it in two steps.
First put them into groups, the ones with fewest digits first:

(all the 2-digit ones,   then all the 3-digit ones,   then all the 4-digit ones etc.)
| 12  84  32  75 |  | 623  486 |  | 4,563   2,143 |

② Then just put each separate group in order of size:

| 12  32  75  84 |  | 486   623 |  | 2,143   4,563 |

For decimals do the whole-number bit first before looking at what's after the point.
With numbers between 0 and 1, first group them by the number of 0s at the start.
The group with the most 0s at the start comes first, just like this:

(those with 2 initial 0s,   then those with 1 initial 0,   then those with no initial 0s.)
| 0.0026  0.007 |  | 0.03  0.098 |  | 0.14   0.531   0.7 |

Once they're in groups, just order them by comparing the first <u>non-zero</u> digits.
(If the first digits are the same, look at the next digit along instead.)

## Rounding Whole Numbers

The easiest ways to round off a number are:
1) "<u>To the nearest WHOLE NUMBER</u>"      3) "<u>To the nearest HUNDRED</u>".
2) "<u>To the nearest TEN</u>"      4) "<u>To the nearest THOUSAND</u>"

This isn't difficult so long as you remember the *2 RULES*:

> 1) The number <u>always lies between 2 POSSIBLE ANSWERS</u>,
>    Just <u>choose the one it's NEAREST TO</u>.
> 2) If the number is <u>exactly in the MIDDLE</u>, then <u>ROUND IT UP</u>.

<u>EXAMPLES</u>:

**1) Give 231 to the nearest <u>TEN</u>.**
  *ANSWER*:  231 is between 230 and 240, but it is nearer to <u>230</u>

**2) Round 45.7 to the nearest <u>WHOLE NUMBER</u>.**
  *ANSWER*: 45.7 is between 45 and 46, but it is nearer to <u>46</u>

**3) Round 4500 to the nearest <u>THOUSAND</u>.**
  *ANSWER*: 4500 is between 4000 and 5000.  In fact it is *exactly halfway*
  between them.  <u>So we ROUND IT UP</u> (see Rule 2 above) to <u>5000</u>

## The Acid Test:

*0.008, 0.09, 0.1, 0.2, 0.307, 0.37*

1) Write these numbers in ascending order:  0.37  0.008  0.307  0.1  0.09  0.2
2) Round these off to the nearest 10:  a) 453  b) 682  c) 46.2  d) 14

# Negative Numbers

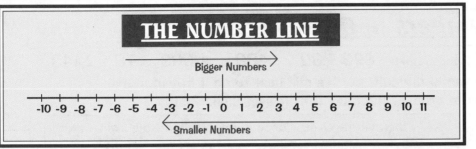

**THE NUMBER LINE**

Bigger Numbers →

-10 -9 -8 -7 -6 -5 -4 -3 -2 -1 0 1 2 3 4 5 6 7 8 9 10 11

← Smaller Numbers

You need to *remember* this diagram of <u>THE NUMBER LINE</u> — it could be the answer to all your problems — well, all your *negative number problems* anyway.

## 1) Putting Negative Numbers in Order

<u>EXAMPLE</u>:  <u>Put these in order of size</u>:    12,  -4,  5,  -2,  10,  -11,  2,  -7
ANS:         *1) Quickly <u>draw out the full Number Line</u> as shown below*
             *2) Put the numbers <u>in the same order as they appear on the number line</u>.*

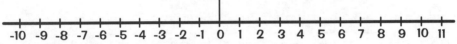

-10 -9 -8 -7 -6 -5 -4 -3 -2 -1 0 1 2 3 4 5 6 7 8 9 10 11

So in order of size they are:   <u>-11,  -7,  -4,  -2,  2,  5,  10,  12</u>

> <u>Note that</u> -4 is **BIGGER** than -7, because it is **FURTHER UP THE NUMBER LINE**.
> <u>Negative numbers go the "wrong way"</u> — smaller numbers are bigger!

## 2) Finding The Range of Values

A common Exam question is for the <u>temperature range</u> of a place where it is below freezing at night.

> <u>EXAMPLE</u>: One day the temperatures in Moscow were:     Midday — 7°C
>                                                            Midnight — -15°C
>                     What was the full <u>RANGE</u> of temperature?

<u>ANSWER</u>: Once again, just do a <u>quick sketch of the Number Line</u>, mark the two temperatures on it and then just <u>count how many degrees it is between them</u> — easy:

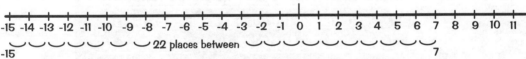

-15 -14 -13 -12 -11 -10 -9 -8 -7 -6 -5 -4 -3 -2 -1 0 1 2 3 4 5 6 7 8 9 10 11
-15 ⌣⌣⌣⌣⌣⌣⌣ ⌣ ⌣ 22 places between ⌣⌣⌣⌣⌣⌣⌣⌣ 7

The answer is:  The full range of temperature in Moscow was <u>22°C</u>.

## 3) Multiplying and Dividing

For *multiplying and dividing with* **NEGATIVE NUMBERS** these rules apply:

| + | + | makes | + |
|---|---|-------|---|
| + | − | makes | − |
| − | + | makes | − |
| − | − | makes | + |

e.g.  -4 × 3 = -12     ( − and + makes −)
        5 × -6 = -30     ( + and − makes −)
       -12 ÷ 2 = -6     ( − and + makes −)
       -5 × -8 = +40    ( − and − makes +)

# The Acid Test:

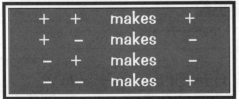

1) Arrange these in order of size:  -5,  4,  10,  -1,  7,  -12,  45,  -23,  -22,  0
2) One day the temperature went from -9°C to 12°C.  What was the rise in temperature?
3) Work these two out without your calculator:  a) -3 × 5    b) -20 ÷ -4

# _Prime Numbers_

## 1) _Basically, PRIME Numbers don't divide by anything_

And that's the <u>best way to think of them</u>.
So <u>Prime Numbers</u> are all the numbers that <u>DON'T come up in Times Tables</u>:

| 2 | 3 | 5 | 7 | 11 | 13 | 17 | 19 | 23 | 29 | 31 | 37 | ... |

As you can see, they're an <u>awkward-looking bunch</u> (that's because they don't divide by anything!).   For example:

| _The only numbers_ that multiply to give 7 are | $1 \times 7$ |
| _The only numbers_ that multiply to give 31 are | $1 \times 31$ |

In fact the <u>only way</u> to get <u>ANY PRIME NUMBER</u> is         $1 \times$ ITSELF

## 2) _They All End in 1, 3, 7 or 9_

1) <u>1 is NOT a prime number</u>

2) The first four prime numbers are  <u>2, 3, 5 and 7</u>

3) <u>2 and 5 are the EXCEPTIONS</u>  because
        <u>all the rest</u> end in <u>1, 3, 7 or 9</u>

4) But <u>NOT ALL</u> numbers ending in <u>1, 3, 7 or 9</u>
        are primes, as shown here:
   (Only the _circled ones_ are _primes_)

②  ③  ⑤  ⑦
⑪  ⑬  ⑰  ⑲
21  ㉓  27  ㉙
㉛  33  ㊲  39
㊸  ㊸  ㊼  49
51  ㊿  57  ㊾
㊶  63  ㊿  69

## 3) _How to Find Prime Numbers_   — _a very simple method_

1) _Since all primes_ (above 5) <u>end in 1, 3, 7, or 9</u>, then to find a prime number between say, 70 and 80, <u>the only possibilities</u> are:  <u>71, 73, 77 and 79</u>

2) Now, to find which of them <u>ACTUALLY ARE</u> primes you only need to <u>divide each one by 3 and 7</u>.  If it doesn't divide exactly by either 3 or 7 then it's a prime.
        (This simple rule <u>using just 3 and 7</u> is true for checking primes <u>up to 120</u>)

<u>So, to find the primes between 70 and 80, just try dividing 71, 73, 77 and 79 by 3 and 7:</u>

$71 \div 3 = 23.667$,          $71 \div 7 = 10.143$       so <u>71 _IS_ a prime number</u>
                                                              (_because it ends in 1, 3, 7 or 9 and it <u>doesn't divide by 3 or 7</u>_)

$73 \div 3 = 24.333$,          $73 \div 7 = 10.429$       so <u>73 _IS_ a prime number</u>

$79 \div 3 = 26.333$          $79 \div 7 = 11.286$       so <u>79 _IS_ a prime number</u>

$77 \div 3 = 25.667$    <u>BUT</u>:  $77 \div 7 = \underline{11}$ — 11 is a <u>whole number</u> (or 'integer'),
                        so <u>77 is NOT a prime</u>, because it will <u>divide by 7</u> ($7 \times 11 = 77$)

## _The Acid Test:_         LEARN the main points in <u>ALL 3 SECTIONS</u> above.

Now <u>cover the page and write down</u> everything you've just learned.
1) Write down the first 15 prime numbers (_without_ looking them up).
2) Using the above method, find all the prime numbers between 90 and 110.

# Multiples, Factors and Prime Factors

## Multiples

The **MULTIPLES** of a number are simply its **TIMES TABLE**:

E.g. the <u>multiples of 13</u> are    13  26  39  52  65  78  91  104  ...

## Factors

The **FACTORS** (or **DIVIDERS**) of a number are all the numbers that **DIVIDE INTO IT**.   There's a special way to find them:

### Example 1:    "Find **ALL** the factors of 24".

Start off with 1× the number itself, then try 2×, then 3× and so on, listing the pairs in rows like this.  Try each one in turn and put a dash if it doesn't divide exactly.  Eventually, when you get a number *repeated*,  you *stop*.

Increasing by 1 each time

$1 \times 24$
$2 \times 12$
$3 \times 8$
$4 \times 6$
$5 \times -$
$6 \times 4$

So the **FACTORS OF 24** are  <u>1,2,3,4,6,8,12,24</u>

This method guarantees you find them **ALL** — but *don't forget 1 and 24!*

## Factors    Example 2:    "Find the factors of 64".

Check each one in turn, to see if it divides or not. Use your calculator when you can, if you're not totally confident.

$1 \times 64$
$2 \times 32$
$3 \times -$
$4 \times 16$
$5 \times -$
$6 \times -$
$7 \times -$
$8 \times 8$ — The 8 has *repeated* so *stop here*.

So the **FACTORS of 64** are  <u>1,2,4,8,16,32,64</u>

# Finding Prime Factors — The Factor Tree

Any number can be broken down into <u>a string of</u> <u>PRIME NUMBERS</u> (see P.3) <u>all multiplied together</u> — this is called "<u>Expressing it as a product of prime factors</u>", and to be honest it's pretty tedious – but it's in the Exam, <u>and it's not difficult so long as you know what it is</u>.

The mildly entertaining "<u>Factor Tree</u>" method is best, where you start at the top and split your number off into factors as shown.  Each time you get a prime, you <u>ring it</u> and you finally end up with <u>all the prime factors</u>, which you can then arrange <u>in order</u>.

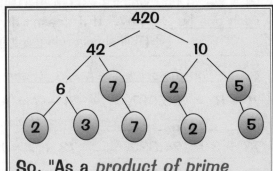

So, "As a *product of prime factors*", <u>420 = 2×2×3×5×7</u>

## The Acid Test:

**LEARN** what <u>Multiples, Factors and Prime Factors</u> are, AND HOW TO FIND THEM.   <u>Turn over and write it down.</u>

Then try these <u>without the notes</u>:
1) List the first 10 multiples of 7, and the first 10 multiples of 9.
2) List <u>all</u> the factors of 36 and <u>all</u> the factors of 84.
3) Express as a product of prime factors:    a) 990    b) 160.

# LCM and HCF

Two big fancy names, but don't be put off — they're both _real easy._

## LCM — "_Least Common Multiple_"

"_Least Common Multiple_" — sure, it sounds kind of complicated but _all it means is this_:

> The **_SMALLEST_** number that will **_DIVIDE BY_**
> **_ALL_** the numbers in question.

**Method**
1) _LIST_ the _MULTIPLES_ of _ALL_ the numbers.
2) Find the _SMALLEST_ one that's in _ALL the lists_.
3) Easy peasy innit.

**Example** _Find the least common multiple (LCM) of 6 and 7_

**Answer**
Multiples of 6 are:   6, 12, 18, 24, 30, 36, (42,) 48, 54, 60, 66, ...
Multiples of 7 are:   7, 14, 21, 28, 35, (42,) 49, 56, 63, 70, 77, ...

> So the _least common multiple_ (LCM) of 6 and 7 is _42_.
> Told you it was easy.

## HCF — "_Highest Common Factor_"

"_Highest Common Factor_" — all it means is _this_:

> The **_BIGGEST_** number that will **_DIVIDE INTO_**
> **_ALL_** the numbers in question.

**Method**
1) _LIST_ the _FACTORS_ of _all_ the numbers.
2) Find the _BIGGEST_ one that's in _ALL the lists_.
3) Easy peasy innit.

**Example** _Find the highest common factor (HCF) of 36, 54, and 72_

**Answer**
Factors of 36 are:   1, 2, 3, 4, 6, 9, 12, (18,) 36
Factors of 54 are:   1, 2, 3, 6, 9, (18,) 27, 54
Factors of 72 are:   1, 2, 3, 4, 6, 8, 9, 12, (18,) 24, 36, 72

> So the _highest common factor_ (HCF) of 36, 54 and 72 is _18_.
> Told you it was easy.

Just _take care_ listing the factors — make sure you use the _proper method_ (as shown on the previous page) or you'll miss one and blow the whole thing out of the water.

## The Acid Test:
LEARN what _LCM and HCF_ are, AND HOW TO FIND THEM.   _Turn over and write it all down._

1) List the first 10 multiples of 8, and the first 10 multiples of 9.   What's their LCM?
2) List _all_ the factors of 56 and _all_ the factors of 104.   What's their HCF?
3) What's the Least Common Multiple of 7 and 9?
4) What's the Highest Common Factor of 36 and 84?

# Special Number Sequences

## 1) EVEN NUMBERS   …all Divide by 2

2  4  6  8  10  12  14  16  18  20 …

All *EVEN* numbers **END** in <u>0, 2, 4, 6 or 8</u>

e.g. 200, 342, 576, 94

## 2) ODD NUMBERS   …**DON'T** divide by 2

1  3  5  7  9  11  13  15  17  19  21 …

All *ODD* numbers **END** in <u>1, 3, 5, 7 or 9</u>

e.g. 301, 95, 807, 43

## 3) SQUARE NUMBERS:

They're called *SQUARE NUMBERS* because they're like the areas of this pattern of squares:

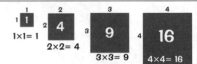

(1×1) (2×2) (3×3) (4×4) (5×5) (6×6) (7×7) (8×8) (9×9) (10×10) (11×11) (12×12) (13×13) (14×14) (15×15)

| 1 | 4 | 9 | 16 | 25 | 36 | 49 | 64 | 81 | 100 | 121 | 144 | 169 | 196 | 225... |

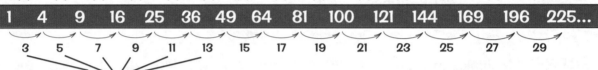

3   5   7   9   11   13   15   17   19   21   23   25   27   29

Note that the <u>DIFFERENCES</u> between the <u>square numbers</u> are all the <u>ODD</u> numbers.

## 4) CUBE NUMBERS:

They're called *CUBE NUMBERS* because they're like the volumes of this pattern of cubes.

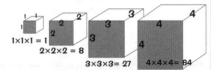

(1x1x1) (2x2x2) (3x3x3) (4x4x4) (5x5x5)  (6x6x6)   (7x7x7)   (8x8x8)   (9x9x9)  (10x10x10)…

| 1 | 8 | 27 | 64 | 125 | 216 | 343 | 512 | 729 | 1000... |

Admit it, you never knew maths could be this exciting did you!

## 5) POWERS:

Powers are "numbers *multiplied by themselves* so many times".

"*Two to the power three*" = $2^3$ = $2 \times 2 \times 2$ = 8

Here's the first few *POWERS OF 2*:

| 2 | 4 | 8 | 16 | 32... |

$2^1=2$  $2^2=4$  $2^3=8$  $2^4=16$  etc…

… and the first *POWERS OF 10* (even easier):

| 10 | 100 | 1000 | 10 000... |

$10^1=10$   $10^2=100$   $10^3=1000$   etc…

## 6) TRIANGLE NUMBERS:

To remember the triangle numbers you have to picture in your mind this *increasing pattern of triangles*, where each new row has <u>one more blob</u> than the previous row.

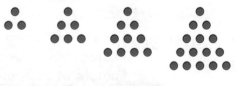

| 1 | 3 | 6 | 10 | 15 | 21 | 28 | 36 | 45 | 55 | .... |

2   3   4   5   6   7   8   9   10   11   12

It's definitely worth learning this simple <u>pattern of differences</u>, as well as the formula for the <u>$n^{th}$ term</u> (see P.23) which is:

$$n^{th} \text{ term} = \tfrac{1}{2} n (n + 1)$$

# The Acid Test:

LEARN the first 10 NUMBERS in all six sequences:
EVEN, ODD, SQUARE, CUBE and TRIANGLE NUMBERS.

1) Cover up the page and then write down the first <u>15</u> numbers in all six sequences.

2) From this list of numbers:   23, 45, 56, 81, 25, 97, 134, 156, 125, 36, 1, 64
write down: a) all the <u>even</u> numbers  b) all the <u>odd</u> numbers  c) all the <u>square</u> numbers
d) all the <u>cube</u> numbers  e) all the <u>powers</u> of 2 or 10.   f) all the <u>triangle</u> numbers.

# Square Roots and Cube Roots

## Square Roots

"<u>Squared</u>" means "<u>times by itself</u>" : $P^2 = P \times P$
— <u>SQUARE ROOT</u> is the <u>reverse process</u>.

The best way to think of it is this:

**"Square Root" means
"What Number Times by Itself gives..."**

*Example:* "<u>Find the square root of 49</u>" (i.e. " Find $\sqrt{49}$ " or "Find $49^{1/2}$ ")

To do this you should say it as: "<u>What number TIMES BY ITSELF gives... 49</u>"

Now, if you ever felt inclined to learn the number sequences on P.6 (like you were told to), then of course you'd know instantly that the answer is 7.

On your calculator, <u>it's easy to find any positive square root</u> using the <u>SQUARE ROOT BUTTON</u>: Press $\sqrt{\phantom{x}}$ 49 = = <u>7</u> (See P.13)

## Square Roots can be Positive or Negative

If you multiply a negative number by itself, you get a positive one (see P.2):

$(-2)^2 = (-2) \times (-2) = 4$ But $2^2 = 4$ as well. (What's going on...)

It's actually quite simple: $\sqrt{4} = +2$ or $-2$

... and that goes for all square roots —

whenever you get a <u>positive square root</u>, you also get a <u>negative one</u>.

## Cube Roots

"<u>Cubed</u>" means "<u>times by itself twice</u>" : $T^3 = T \times T \times T$
— <u>CUBE ROOT</u> is the <u>reverse process</u>.

**"Cube Root" means "What Number
Times by Itself TWICE gives..."**

*Example:* "<u>Find the cube root of 64</u>" (i.e. "Find $\sqrt[3]{64}$ " or "Find $64^{\frac{1}{3}}$")

You should say: "<u>What number TIMES BY ITSELF TWICE gives... 64</u>"

From your in-depth revision of P.6 you will of course know the answer is 4.

<u>OR</u> on your calculator just use the <u>CUBE ROOT BUTTON</u>:

Press $\sqrt[3]{\phantom{x}}$ 27 = = <u>3</u> (See P.13)

## And Don't Forget:

"<u>SOMETHING TO THE POWER ½</u>" is just a different way of asking for a <u>SQUARE ROOT</u> e.g. $81^{1/2}$ is the same as $\sqrt{81}$ which is just <u>9</u>.

"<u>SOMETHING TO THE POWER 1/3</u>" is just a different way of asking for a <u>CUBE ROOT</u> e.g. $27^{\frac{1}{3}}$ is the same as $\sqrt[3]{27}$ which is just <u>3</u>.

## The Acid Test:

<u>LEARN</u> the <u>2 statements</u> in the shaded boxes, the <u>best method for finding roots</u> and what <u>fractional powers</u> mean. Then turn the page and write it all down.

1) Use your calculator to find a) $56^{1/2}$ b) $450^{\frac{1}{3}}$ c) $\sqrt{200}$ d) $\sqrt[3]{8000}$.
   For a) and c), what are the other values that your calculator didn't give?
2) a) If $g^2 = 36$, find g.  b) If $b^3 = 64$, find b.  c) If $4 \times r^2 = 36$, find r.

# _Multiplying and Dividing by 10, 100..._

This is _very simple_.   Just _make sure you know it_ — that's all.

## 1) TO MULTIPLY ANY NUMBER BY 10

> Move the Decimal Point ONE place BIGGER
> and if it's needed, ADD A ZERO on the end.

_Examples:_

$23.6 \times 10 = \underline{236}$

$345 \times 10 = \underline{3450}$

$45.678 \times 10 = \underline{456.78}$

## 2) TO MULTIPLY BY 100, 1000, OR 10,000, the same rule applies:

> Move the Decimal Point
> so many places BIGGER
> and ADD ZEROS if necessary.

_Examples:_

$341 \times 1000 = \underline{341000}$

$2.3542 \times 10,000 = \underline{23542}$

## 3) TO DIVIDE BY A MULTIPLE OF 10, move the d.p. the other way:

> Move the Decimal Point so many
> places SMALLER and REMOVE
> ZEROS after the decimal point.

_Examples:_

$341 \div 1000 = \underline{0.341}$

$23542 \div 10,000 = \underline{2.3542}$

> You always _move_ the _DECIMAL POINT_ this much:
> 1 place for 10,     2 places for 100,
> 3 places for 1000,     4 for 10,000     etc.

## 4) TO MULTIPLY BY NUMBERS LIKE 20, 300, 8000 ETC.

> MULTIPLY by 2 or 3 or 8 etc. FIRST,
> then move the Decimal Point so many places BIGGER ( ↗ )
> according to how many noughts there are.

_Example:_     To find $234 \times 200$, _first multiply by 2_     $234 \times 2 = 468$,
then _move the DP 2 places_          $= \underline{46800}$

## 5) DIVIDING BY 40, 300, 7000 ETC.

> DIVIDE BY 4 or 3 or 7 etc. FIRST
> and then move the Decimal Point so many
> places SMALLER (i.e. to the left ↙ ).

_Example:_     To find $960 \div 300$, _first divide by 3_     $960 \div 3 = 320$,
then _move the DP 2 places smaller_     $= \underline{3.2}$

## _The Acid Test:_

| | | | |
|---|---|---|---|
| 1) Work out | a) $34.5 \times 10$ | b) $9.65 \times 1000$ | c) $2.4 \times 400$ |
| 2) Work out | a) $654.2 \div 100$ | b) $3.08 \div 1000$ | c) $360 \div 30$ |

# Fractions, Decimals and Percentages

The one word that could describe all these three is <u>PROPORTION</u>. Fractions, decimals and percentages are simply <u>three different ways</u> of expressing a <u>proportion</u> of something — and it's pretty important you should see them as <u>closely related and completely interchangeable</u> with each other. This table shows the really common conversions which you should know straight off without having to work them out:

| Fraction | Decimal | Percentage |
|----------|---------|------------|
| 1/2 | 0.5 | 50% |
| 1/4 | 0.25 | 25% |
| 3/4 | 0.75 | 75% |
| 1/3 | 0.333333 | 33% |
| 2/3 | 0.666667 | 67% |
| 1/10 | 0.1 | 10% |
| 2/10 | 0.2 | 20% |
| X/10 | 0.X | X0% |
| 1/5 | 0.2 | 20% |
| 2/5 | 0.4 | 40% |

⅓ and ⅔ have what're known as '<u>recurring</u>' decimals — the same pattern of numbers carries on <u>repeating</u> itself forever. (Except here, the pattern's just a single 3 or a single 6. You could have, for instance: 0.143143143...) The ⅔ decimal ends in a 7 because it's been rounded up.

The more of those conversions you learn, the better — but for those that you <u>don't know</u>, you must <u>also learn</u> how to <u>convert</u> between the three types. These are the methods:

Fraction $\xrightarrow{\text{Divide (use your calculator if you can)}}$ Decimal $\xrightarrow{\times \text{ by 100}}$ Percentage

e.g. ½ is 1÷2    = 0.5    e.g. 0.5 × 100    = 50%

Fraction $\xleftarrow{\text{The tricky one}}$ Decimal $\xleftarrow{\div \text{ by 100}}$ Percentage

<u>Converting decimals to fractions</u> is only possible for <u>exact decimals</u> that haven't been rounded off.

It's simple enough, but it's best illustrated by examples so look now at P.10 and work out what the simple rule is. You should then be able to fill in the rest of this table:

| Fraction | Decimal | Percentage |
|----------|---------|------------|
| 1/5 | | |
| | 0.35 | |
| | | 45% |
| | 0.12 | |
| 1/8 | | |
| | 0.77 | |

# The Acid Test:

LEARN the <u>whole of the top table</u> and the 4 conversion processes for FDP.

Now cover the page and write out the top FDP table from memory, and then the four conversion rules. Then fill in all the spaces in the 2nd table shown above.

# Fractions Without the Calculator

Doing fractions _by hand_ is always a pest... so you'd better learn this little lot _before your exam._

## 1) Converting Fractions to Decimals — Just DIVIDE

Just remember that " / " means " ÷ ", __so ¼ means 1 ÷ 4 = 0.25__

The _denominator_ (bottom number) of a fraction, tells you if it'll be a _recurring_ or _terminating decimal_ when you convert it.

only _prime_ factors: **2 & 5**

also _other_ prime factors

_For prime factors see p.4_

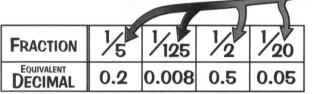

| FRACTION | ⅕ | ¹⁄₁₂₅ | ½ | ¹⁄₂₀ | | ⅟₇ | ⅟₃₅ | ⅓ | ⅙ |
|---|---|---|---|---|---|---|---|---|---|
| EQUIVALENT DECIMAL | 0.2 | 0.008 | 0.5 | 0.05 | | 0.142857 | 0.0285714 | 0.3333 | 0.16666 |

Fractions where the denominator has _prime factors_ of _only 2 or 5_ will give _terminating decimals_. All _other fractions_ will give _recurring decimals_.

## 2) Converting Decimals to Fractions
— it's a simple rule, so work it out yourself!

$0.6 = {}^6/_{10}$,  $0.3 = {}^3/_{10}$,  $0.7 = {}^7/_{10}$,  $0.X = {}^X/_{10}$, etc.

$0.12 = {}^{12}/_{100}$,  $0.78 = {}^{78}/_{100}$,  $0.45 = {}^{45}/_{100}$,  $0.05 = {}^5/_{100}$, etc.

These can then be _cancelled down._

$0.345 = {}^{345}/_{1000}$,  $0.908 = {}^{908}/_{1000}$,  $0.024 = {}^{24}/_{1000}$,  $0.XYZ = {}^{XYZ}/_{1000}$, etc.

And remember — all _recurring_ decimals are just (exact) fractions in disguise.

_By Hand_

## 1) Multiplying — easy
Multiply top and bottom separately:

$$\tfrac{3}{5} \times \tfrac{4}{7} = {}^{3\times4}/_{5\times7} = {}^{12}/_{35}$$

## 2) Dividing — quite easy
Turn the _2nd fraction UPSIDE DOWN_ and then _multiply:_

$$\tfrac{3}{4} \div \tfrac{1}{3} = \tfrac{3}{4} \times \tfrac{3}{1} = {}^{3\times3}/_{4\times1} = {}^9/_4$$

## 3) Adding, subtracting — fraught
Add or subtract _TOP LINES ONLY_
but _only if the bottom numbers are the same._
(If they're not the same it gets very tricky – see opposite.)

$$\tfrac{2}{6} + \tfrac{1}{6} = \tfrac{3}{6}$$

$$\tfrac{5}{7} - \tfrac{3}{7} = \tfrac{2}{7}$$

## 4) Cancelling down — easy
_Divide top and bottom by the same number,_
till they won't go any further:

$$\overset{\div3 \quad \div2}{{}^{18}/_{24} = {}^6/_8 = \tfrac{3}{4}}_{\div3 \quad \div2}$$

## 5) Finding a fraction of something — just multiply.
_Multiply_ the 'something' by the _TOP_ of the fraction,

then _divide_ it by the _BOTTOM_:

$$\frac{9}{20} \text{ of £360} = \{(9) \times £360\} \div (20) = \frac{£3240}{20} = £162$$

or: $\dfrac{9}{20}$ of £360 $= \dfrac{9}{1} \times £360 \times \dfrac{1}{20} = £162$

# More Fractions

## 6) Equalising the Denominator — why oh why...

You need this whether you're using your *calculator or not*. It comes in handy with ordering fractions by size, and you need it for addition and subtraction by hand.

To make the bottom number the same, you need to find a common multiple of all the denominators:

*Example:* Put these fractions in ascending order of size: $\frac{8}{3}$ , $\frac{6}{4}$ , $\frac{12}{5}$

⟹ Least Common Multiple = 3 × 4 × 5 = 60 ⟹ $\frac{8}{3} = \frac{8}{3} \times \frac{20}{20} = \frac{160}{60}$

*See P.5* so put all the fractions over 60... $\frac{6}{4} = \frac{6}{4} \times \frac{15}{15} = \frac{90}{60}$ ⟹ $\frac{90}{60}$ , $\frac{144}{60}$ , $\frac{160}{60}$

(remember that anything divided by itself = 1) $\frac{12}{5} = \frac{12}{5} \times \frac{12}{12} = \frac{144}{60}$ *OR:* $\frac{6}{4}$ , $\frac{12}{5}$ , $\frac{8}{3}$

*When you can though, use your calculator* to do all fractions in your exams. It makes sense...

## The Fraction Button:

Use this as much as possible in the Exam.

It's very easy, so make sure you know how to use it — or you'll lose a lot of marks:

1) **TO ENTER A NORMAL FRACTION** like $\frac{1}{4}$   Just press: **1** $a^b_c$ **4**

2) **TO ENTER A MIXED FRACTION** like $1\frac{3}{5}$   Just press: **1** $a^b_c$ **3** $a^b_c$ **5**

3) **TO DO A REGULAR CALCULATION** such as $\frac{1}{5} \times \frac{3}{4}$

Just press: **1** $a^b_c$ **5** **X** **3** $a^b_c$ **4** **=**

4) **TO REDUCE A FRACTION TO ITS LOWEST TERMS**

Just enter it and then press **=**

e.g. $\frac{9}{12}$ ·   **9** $a^b_c$ **12** **=**    3⌐4 = $\frac{3}{4}$

5) **TO CONVERT BETWEEN MIXED AND TOP-HEAVY FRACTIONS**

Just press **SHIFT** $a^b_c$ e.g. to give $2\frac{3}{8}$ as a top-heavy fraction:

Press: **2** $a^b_c$ **3** $a^b_c$ **8** **=** to enter the fraction, then **SHIFT** $a^b_c$ to convert it to $\frac{19}{8}$.

## The Acid Test:

LEARN the 2 Rules for converting Fractions to Decimals, the 6 Manual Methods and the 5 features of the Fraction Button.

*Then cover up these two pages and write down what you've learned.*

1) Do these *WITH YOUR CALCULATOR*:

a) 1/2 x 3/4   b) 3/5 ÷ 2/9   c) 1/3 + 2/5   d) Find x: $2\frac{3}{5} = \frac{x}{5}$   e) Find y: $\frac{14}{98} = \frac{y}{7}$

f) Convert 3/8 into a decimal    g) Convert 0.035 into a fraction, and cancel it down.

2) Do these *BY HAND*:

a) 2/3 x 4/5   b) 4/5 ÷ 3/10   c) 5/6 – 2/6   d) Express 36/84 in its simplest form.

e) Work out 12/19 × 133.   f) Work out 12/19 × 134. Express your answer as a fraction.

(Pssssssst... what that means is that rather than a decimal of e.g. 1.25, you'd give the answer as 1¼.
Make sure you can do that — 'coz they could ask you it in the Exam.)

# _Percentages_

You shouldn't have any trouble with most percentage questions, especially types 1 and 2 below. Watch out for type 3 questions and make sure you know the proper method for doing them. "Percentage change" can also catch you out if you don't watch all the details.

## _Type 1_
_"Find x% of y"_ — e.g. Find 15% of £46 $\Rightarrow$ 0.15 ×46 = £6.90

## _Type 2_
_"Express x as a percentage of y"_
e.g. Give 40p as a percentage of £3.34 $\Rightarrow$ (40 ÷ 334) × 100 = 12%

## _Type 3_
— _IDENTIFIED BY NOT GIVING THE "ORIGINAL VALUE"_

These are the type most people get wrong – but only because they don't recognise them as a type 3 and don't apply this simple method:

_Example:_ 
> A house increases in value by 20% to £72,000.
> Find what it was worth _before_ the rise.

## _Method_

| | | |
|---|---|---|
| £72,000 | = | 120% |
| £600 | = | 1% |
| £60,000 | = | 100% |

÷120 ↘
×100 ↘

So the original price was £60,000

An INCREASE of 20% means that £72,000 represents _120% of the original_ value. If it was a DROP of 20%, then we would put "£72,000 = 80%" instead, and then divide by 80 on the LHS, instead of 120.

_Always set them out exactly like this example._ The trickiest bit is deciding the top % figure on the RHS — the 2nd and 3rd rows are _always_ 1% and 100%.

## _Percentage Change_

It is common to give a _change in value_ as a _percentage_. This is the formula for doing so — LEARN IT, AND USE IT:

$$\text{PERCENTAGE "CHANGE"} = \frac{\text{"CHANGE"}}{\text{ORIGINAL}} \times 100$$

By "change", we could mean all sorts of things such as: "Profit", "loss", "appreciation", "depreciation", "increase", "decrease", "error", "discount", etc. For example,

$$\text{percentage "profit"} = \frac{\text{"profit"}}{\text{original}} \times 100$$

Note the great importance of using the ORIGINAL VALUE in this formula.

## _The Acid Test:_
LEARN The details for TYPE 3 QUESTIONS and PERCENTAGE CHANGE, then _turn over and write it all down._

1) A trader buys watches for £5 and sells them for £7. Find his profit as a percentage.
2) A car depreciates by 30% to £14,350. What was it worth before?
3) Find the percentage error in rounding 3.452 to 3.5. Give your answer to 2 DP.

# Calculator Buttons 1

The next few pages are full of lovely calculator tricks to save you a lot of button-bashing.

## Two tricks for Reading Displayed Answers

### 1) Putting "× 10" in for Numbers that are too big

Sometimes your answer will be too big for the calculator display and instead you'll get two extra little numbers up in the air at the end of the display like this:

$$4.567^{\,13}$$

To give this as a proper answer *you have to remember to put "× 10" into your answer* like this:  $4.567 \times 10^{13}$.  So don't forget!

### 2) Remembering that your answer is in £ and Pence

You have to think carefully what the display actually means.  Look at these examples:

A display showing  `3.6`  means the answer is £3.60

A display showing  `0.54`  means the answer is 54p

A display showing  `2.546453`  means the answer is £2.55

## 1) Entering Negative Numbers

Some calculators have a `+/−` button which you press *after* you've entered the number. Others just have a minus button `(−)` which you press *before* entering the number.

So to work out − 5 × − 6 you'd either press...  `(−)` `5` `×` `(−)` `6` `=`

or...  `5` `+/−` `×` `6` `+/−` `=`

Why can't they all just be the same... (The examples in this book will use the `(−)` button.)

## 2) Square, Square Root and Cube Root

The SQUARE, SQUARE ROOT, and CUBE ROOT buttons are `x²` `√` and `³√` .

1) The `x²` button squares the number you typed, i.e. IT MULTIPLIES IT BY ITSELF.
It's ideal for finding the area of a circle, using the well-known (hah!) formula:

$A = \pi r^2$  e.g.  if r = 5 then press `3.14` `×` `5` `x²` `=` which gives you 78.5.

(To get a more accurate answer, use the π button which is usually the second function of the EXP key)

2) `√` is the REVERSE PROCESS of `x²` — it calculates the SQUARE ROOT of the number you

enter.  Pressing `√` `25` `=` gives `5` ,

then `x²` `=` takes you back to `25`

3) `³√` gives the CUBE ROOT (See P.7) which is the reverse of CUBING a number.

E.g. `³√` `27` `=` gives `3` ,

then pressing `x³` `=` takes you back to `27` .

## 3) The Powers Button:

It's used for working out powers of numbers quickly.  For example to find $7^5$, instead of pressing 7×7×7×7×7 you should just press `7` `xʸ` `5` `=`

# Calculator Buttons 2

## 4) The MEMORY BUTTONS ([STO] Store, [RCL] Recall)

(On some calculators the memory buttons are called [Min] (memory in) and [MR] (memory recall)).
Contrary to popular belief, the memory is not intended for storing your favourite phone number, but in fact is a mighty useful feature for keeping a number you've just calculated, so you can use it again shortly afterwards.

For something like $\dfrac{16}{15+12SIN40}$, you could just

work out the *bottom line* first and *stick it in the memory*:

*Never* round off part way through a calculation. It's easy to avoid doing this by using the memory function.

Press [15] [+] [12] [SIN] [40] [=] and then [STO] (Or [STO] [M] or [STO] [1] or [Min] )
to keep the result of the bottom line in the memory.
Then you simply press [16] [÷] [RCL] [=], and the answer is 0.7044.
(Instead of [RCL], you might need to type [RCL] [M] or [RCL] [1] or [MR] on yours.)

Once you've practised with the memory buttons a bit, you'll soon find them very useful.
They can speed things up no end.

## 5) Bodmas and the Brackets Buttons

The BRACKETS BUTTONS are [ ( ] and [ ) ].

One of the biggest problems people have with their calculators is not realising that the calculator always works things out IN A CERTAIN ORDER, which is summarised by the word BODMAS (see P.16), which stands for:

Brackets, Other, Division, Multiplication, Addition, Subtraction

This becomes really important when you want to work out even a simple thing like $\dfrac{23+45}{64\times3}$

— it's no good just pressing [23] [+] [45] [÷] [64] [×] [3] [=] — it will be completely

underline. The calculator will think you mean $23+\dfrac{45}{64}\times3$ because the calculator will do the

*division and multiplication* BEFORE it does the *addition*.

The secret is to OVERRIDE the automatic BODMAS order of operations using the BRACKETS BUTTONS. Brackets are the ultimate priority in BODMAS, which means anything in brackets is worked out before anything else happens to it.
So all you have to do is:

| 1) Write a couple of pairs of brackets into the expression: | $\dfrac{(23+45)}{(64\times3)}$ |
|---|---|

| 2) Then just type it as it's written: | [ ( ] [23] [+] [45] [ ) ] [÷] [ ( ] [64] [×] [3] [ ) ] [=] |
|---|---|

You might think it's difficult to know where to put the brackets in. It's not that difficult, you just put them in pairs around each group of numbers. It's OK to have brackets within other brackets too, e.g. (4 + (5÷2)) As a rule, you can't cause trouble by putting too many brackets in, SO LONG AS THEY ALWAYS GO IN PAIRS.

## 6) The Fraction Button: [ $a\frac{b}{c}$ ]

It's absolutely essential that you learn how to use this button. Full details are given on P.11.

# *Making Formulas From Words*

These can seem a bit confusing but they're not as bad as they look once you know the "tricks of the trade" as it were. There are two main types.

## *Type 1*

In this type there are *instructions about what to do with a number* and you have to *write it as a formula*. The only things they're likely to want you to do in the formula are:

**1) Multiply X     2) Divide X     3) Square X ($X^2$)     4) Add or subtract a number**

**EXAMPLE 1:** *" To find Y, multiply X by three and then subtract four"*

ANSWER:     Start with **X**     $\rightarrow$     **3X**     $\rightarrow$     **3X – 4**     so  **Y = 3X – 4**

Times it by 3     Subtract 4     (not too gruelling)

**EXAMPLE 2:** This is the most difficult you'd ever get:

*"To find Y, square X, divide this by three and then subtract seven. Write a formula for Y."*

ANSWER:     Start with **X**     $\rightarrow$     **$X^2$**     $\rightarrow$     $\dfrac{X^2}{3}$     $\rightarrow$     $\dfrac{X^2}{3} - 7$

Square it     Divide it by 3     Subtract 7

They're not that bad, are they?

$$Y = \dfrac{x^2}{3} - 7$$

## *Type 2*

This is a bit harder. *You have to make up a formula* by putting in letters like "C" for *"cost"* or "n" for *"number of something-or-others"*. Although it may look confusing the formulas always turn out to be REALLY SIMPLE, so make sure you give it a go.

EXAMPLE: Froggatt's deep-fry "CHOCCO-BURGERS" (chocolate-covered beef burgers — not available in all areas) cost 58 pence each. Write a formula for the total cost, **T**, of buying  n  "CHOCCO-BURGERS" at 58p each.

Answer:     **T** stands for the total cost
n  stands for the number of "CHOCCO-BURGERS"

In words the formula is:     Total Cost = Number of "CHOCCO-BURGERS" $\times$ 58p

Putting the letters in:     **T** = n $\times$ 58     or to write it better:  **T = 58n**

## *The Acid Test:*

1) The value of Y is found by taking X, multiplying it by five and then subtracting three. Write down a formula for Y in terms of X.

2) One of Froggatt's main competitors are "Hobnails", who produce a vast range of products including their widely-acclaimed "Hobnail Soup" which costs 95p a tin. Write a formula for the total cost C pence of buying n tins of Hobnail Soup.

# Substituting Values into Formulas

## This topic is a lot easier than you think!

$$C = \frac{5}{9}(F - 32)$$

Generally speaking, algebra is a pretty grim subject, but you should realise that some bits of it are VERY easy, and this is <u>definitely the easiest bit of all</u>, so whatever you do, <u>don't pass up on these easy Exam marks</u>.

## Method

**If you don't follow this STRICT METHOD you'll just keep getting them wrong — it's as simple as that.**

1) <u>Write out the Formula</u>                              e.g  $F = \frac{9}{5}C + 32$

2) <u>Write it again</u>, directly underneath,                     $F = \frac{9}{5}15 + 32$
   but <u>substituting numbers for letters</u> on the RHS.
   <small>(Right Hand Side)</small>

3) Work it out <u>IN STAGES</u>.                               $F = 27 + 32$
   Use <u>BODMAS</u> to work things out <u>IN THE RIGHT ORDER</u>.      $= 59$
   <u>WRITE DOWN</u> values for each bit <u>as you go along</u>.          $\underline{F = 59°}$

4) <u>DO NOT</u> attempt to do it <u>all in one go</u> on your calculator.
   That ridiculous method <u>fails a lot of the time</u>!

## BODMAS

### <u>B</u>rackets, <u>O</u>ther, <u>D</u>ivision, <u>M</u>ultiplication, <u>A</u>ddition, <u>S</u>ubtraction

BODMAS tells you the ORDER in which these operations should be done: Work out <u>brackets</u> first, then <u>Other</u> things like squaring, then <u>multiply</u> / <u>divide</u> groups of numbers before <u>adding</u> or <u>subtracting</u> them.  This set of rules works really well for simple cases, so remember the word:  <u>BODMAS</u>                              (See P.14)

## Example

A mysterious quantity T, is given by:   $T = (P - 7)^2 + 4R/Q$
Find the value of T when P = 4, Q = -2 and R = 3

<u>ANSWER:</u>

1) Write down the formula:        $T = (P - 7)^2 + 4R/Q$

2) Put the numbers in:            $T = (4 - 7)^2 + 4 \times 3/\text{-}2$

3) Then work it out <u>in stages</u> :      $= (-3)^2 + 12/\text{-}2$
                                 $= 9 + \text{-}6$
                                 $= 9 - 6 = \underline{3}$

<u>Note BODMAS in operation:</u>

<u>Brackets</u> worked out first, then <u>squared</u>.  <u>Multiplications</u> and <u>divisions</u> done <u>before</u> finally <u>adding</u> and <u>subtracting</u>.

## The Acid Test:

**<u>LEARN</u> the <u>4 Steps</u> of the Substitution Method and the <u>full meaning</u> of BODMAS.  Then turn over.....**

... and write it all down from memory.    1) Practise the above example until you can do it easily without help.    2) If $C = \frac{5}{9}(F - 32)$, find the value of C when F = 77.

# Basic Algebra

## 1) Terms

Before you can do anything else, you
MUST understand what a TERM is:

1) A TERM IS A COLLECTION OF NUMBERS, LETTERS AND BRACKETS, ALL MULTIPLIED/DIVIDED TOGETHER.

2) TERMS are SEPARATED BY + AND − SIGNS    e.g.    $4x^2 - 3py - 5 + 3p$

3) TERMS always have a + or − ATTACHED TO THE FRONT OF THEM

4) e.g.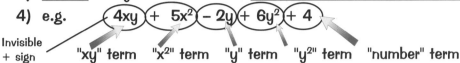

Invisible
+ sign

"xy" term    "x²" term    "y" term    "y²" term    "number" term

> **LEARN THESE THREE DEFINITIONS:**
>
> i)   An EXPRESSION is a bunch of terms joined together.
> ii)  An EQUATION is an expression with an EQUALS SIGN in it,
>      e.g.  $3x^2 + 5x - 7$  is an expression,
>            $3x^2 + 5x - 7 = 2x + 1$  is an equation.
> iii) An IDENTITY is an equation that works for ALL VALUES OF ITS VARIABLES.
>      It's usually written with a ≡ instead of an equals sign.

## 2) Simplifying          "Collecting Like Terms"

*EXAMPLE:*       "Simplify   $2x - 4 + 5x + 6$"

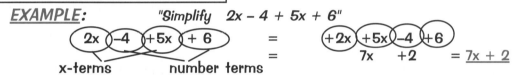

x-terms        number terms

1) Put bubbles round each term, — be sure you *capture the +/− sign* IN FRONT of each.
2) Then you can *move the bubbles into the best order* so that LIKE TERMS *are together*.
3) "LIKE TERMS" have exactly the same combination of letters, e.g. "x-terms" or "xy-terms".
4) Combine LIKE TERMS using the NUMBER LINE (not the other rule for negative numbers).

## 3) Multiplying out Brackets

1) The thing OUTSIDE the brackets multiplies each separate term INSIDE the brackets.
2) When letters are multiplied together, they are just written next to each other, pq.
3) Remember, $R \times R = R^2$, and $TY^2$ means $T \times Y \times Y$, whilst $(TY)^2$ means $T \times T \times Y \times Y$.
4) Remember a minus outside the bracket REVERSES ALL THE SIGNS when you multiply.

### Examples:
1)  $3(2x + 5) = 6x + 15$    2)  $-4(3p^2 - 7q^3) = -12p^2 + 28q^3$

## 4) Cancelling Algebraic Fractions

This is exactly the same as cancelling ordinary fractions.

1) Look for any bits that look the same (common factors) that are on *both the top and the bottom*.
2) Cancel them.

### Example:
Simplify:  $\dfrac{6x(x+4)(x-1)}{3x(x-1)}$    Answer:  $\dfrac{2\cancel{6}\cancel{x}(x+4)\cancel{(x-1)}}{\cancel{3}\cancel{x}\cancel{(x-1)}} = 2(x+4)$

# Basic Algebra

## 5) Expanding and Simplifying

### a) With DOUBLE BRACKETS — you get 4 terms after multiplying

them out and usually 2 of them combine to leave 3 terms, like this:

$$(2P - 4)(3P + 1) = (2P \times 3P) + (2P \times 1) + (-4 \times 3P) + (-4 \times 1)$$
$$= 6P^2 + 2P - 12P - 4$$
$$= \underline{6P^2 - 10P - 4}$$ (these 2 combine together)

### b) SQUARED BRACKETS: e.g. $(3d + 5)^2$ ALWAYS write these out as

two brackets: $(3d + 5)(3d + 5)$ and work them out CAREFULLY like this:

$$(3d + 5)(3d + 5) = 9d^2 + 15d + 15d + 25 = \underline{9d^2 + 30d + 25}$$

YOU SHOULD ALWAYS GET FOUR TERMS from squared brackets, and inevitably _two of these_ will combine together to leave THREE TERMS IN THE END, as shown above.

(The usual WRONG ANSWER, by the way, is $(3d + 5)^2 = 9d^2 + 25$ — eeek!)

## 6) Factorising — putting brackets in

This is the _exact reverse_ of multiplying out brackets. Here's the method to follow:

> 1) Take out the biggest **NUMBER** that goes into all the terms.
>
> 2) Take each letter in turn and take out the highest power (e.g. x, $x^2$ etc) that will go into EVERY term.
>
> 3) Open the brackets and fill in all the bits needed to reproduce each term.

EXAMPLE: Factorise $15x^4y + 20x^2y^3z - 35x^3yz^2$

Answer: $5x^2y(3x^2 + 4y^2z - 7xz^2)$

Biggest number that'll divide into 15, 20 and 35

Highest powers of x and y that will go into _all three terms_

z wasn't in ALL terms so it can't come out as a _common factor_

REMEMBER:

> 1) The bits _taken out_ and put at the front are the _COMMON FACTORS_.
> 2) The bits _inside the brackets_ are _what's needed to get back to the original terms_ if you were to multiply the brackets out again.

## The Acid Test:

LEARN the important details for each of the 6 sections on these 2 pages, then turn over and write it all down.

Then apply the methods to these:

1) Simplify: a) $5x + 3y - 4 - 2y - x$   b) $4k + 3y^2 - 6k + y^2 + 2$   c) $\dfrac{2(x+1)^2}{(x+1)}$

2) Expand: a) $2pq(3p - 4q^2)$   b) $(2g + 5)(4g - 2)$   c) $(4 - 3h)^2$

3) Factorise: a) $14x^2y^3 + 21xy^2 - 35x^3y^4$   b) $12h^2j^3 + 6h^4j^2k - 36h^3jk$

# Laws of Algebra

Mathematicians have a nasty habit of making easy things sound complicated.
These three rules are _really_ simple, but you need to learn the proper names for them.

## The Commutative Law

**THE COMMUTATIVE LAW:** when you're doing addition or multiplication, it doesn't matter which way round you write the numbers.

_EXAMPLES:_    Addition:

$4 + 6 = 10$  and  $6 + 4 = 10$

Multiplication:

$2 \times 6 = 12$  and  $6 \times 2 = 12$

BUT — This law doesn't work for subtraction and division:

_EXAMPLES:_    Subtraction:

$7 - 2 = 5$  but  $2 - 7 = -5$

They are not the same.

Division:

$10 \div 2 = 5$  but  $2 \div 10 = \frac{1}{5}$

They are not the same.

## The Associative Law

**THE ASSOCIATIVE LAW:** when you're adding or multiplying 3 numbers, it doesn't matter where you put the brackets.

_EXAMPLES:_    Addition:

"Work out $2 + 8 + 3$":

$(2 + 8) + 3 = 13$
$2 + (8 + 3) = 13$

Multiplication:

"Work out $5 \times 2 \times 3$":

$(5 \times 2) \times 3 = 30$
$5 \times (2 \times 3) = 30$

## The Distributive Law

**THE DISTRIBUTIVE LAW:** when there are brackets containing an addition and/or a subtraction and there's a number outside, multiplying the brackets, the factor is 'distributed' so it multiplies all the numbers inside.

_EXAMPLE:_    "Work out $10(4 + 5 - 6)$":

$10(4 + 5 - 6)$  can also be written as
$(10 \times 4) + (10 \times 5) - (10 \times 6) = 40 + 50 - 60 = 30$    or can be worked out as:
$10(9 - 6) = 10 \times 3 = 30$

# Solving Equations the Easy Way

The "proper" way to solve equations is shown on P.21. In practice the "proper way" can be pretty difficult so there's a lot to be said for the much easier methods shown below.

The drawback with these is that you can't always use them on very complicated equations. In most Exam questions though, they do just fine.

## 1) THE "COMMON SENSE" APPROACH

The trick here is to realise that the unknown quantity "X" is after all just a number and the "equation" is just a cryptic clue to help you find it

**Example:**     "Solve this equation:   $3X + 4 = 46$"

(i.e. find what number **X** is)

**Answer:**     This is what you should say to yourself:

"Something + 4 = 46"   hmm, so that "something" must be 42.

So that means $3X = 42$, which means "3 times something = 42"

So it must be $42 \div 3$ which is 14        so $\underline{X = 14}$ "

In other words don't think of it as algebra, but as "Find the mystery number".

## 2) THE TRIAL AND ERROR METHOD

This is a perfectly good method, and although it won't work every time, it usually does, especially if the answer is a _whole number_.

The _big secret of trial and error_ methods is to find TWO OPPOSITE CASES and keep taking values IN BETWEEN them.

In other words, find a number that makes the RHS bigger, and then one that makes the LHS bigger, and then try values _in between them_.  (You come back to this in Stage 2 — P.49)

**Example:**     "Solve for X:   $3X + 5 = 21 - 5X$"

(i.e. find the number X)

**Answer:**

Try X=1:      $3 + 5 = 21 - 5$,     $8 = 16$ — no good, RHS too big

Try X=3:      $9 + 5 = 21 - 15$,   $14 = 6$ — no good, now LHS too big

SO TRY IN BETWEEN:  X = 2:   $6 + 5 = 21 - 10$,  $11 = 11$,        YES, so $\underline{X = 2}$.

## The Acid Test:
LEARN these two methods until you can turn the page and write them down with an example for each.

1) Solve:  $4x - 12 = 20$    2) Solve:  $3x + 5 = 5x - 9$

# Solving Equations

_Solving Equations_ means finding the value of x from something like:   $3x + 5 = 4 - 5x$.
Now, not a lot of people know this, but _exactly the same method applies_ to both _solving equations_ and _rearranging formulas_.

1) EXACTLY THE SAME METHOD APPLIES TO BOTH FORMULAS AND EQUATIONS.
2) THE SAME SEQUENCE OF STEPS APPLIES EVERY TIME.

To illustrate the sequence of steps we'll use this equation:   $\sqrt{2 - \dfrac{x+4}{2x+5}} = 3$

## The Six Steps Applied to Equations

1) Get rid of any square root signs by <u>squaring both sides</u>:   $2 - \dfrac{x+4}{2x+5} = 9$

2) Get everything off the bottom by
<u>cross-multiplying up to EVERY OTHER TERM</u>:

$$2 - \frac{x+4}{2x+5} = 9 \quad \Rightarrow \quad 2(2x+5) - (x+4) = 9(2x+5)$$

3) Multiply out any brackets:   $4x + 10 - x - 4 = 18x + 45$

4) Collect all <u>subject terms</u> on one side of the "=" and all <u>non-subject terms</u> on the other side, <u>remembering to reverse the +/− sign of any term that crosses the "="</u> :

+18x moves across the "=" and becomes -18x
+10 moves across the "=" and becomes -10
-4 moves across the "=" and becomes +4

$$4x - x - 18x = 45 - 10 + 4$$

5) <u>Combine together like terms</u> on each side of the equation, and reduce it to the form "<u>Ax = B</u>", where A and B are just numbers (or bunches of letters in the case of formulas):

$$-15x = 39$$
( "Ax = B":   A = -15,  B = 39,  x is the subject )

6) Finally <u>slide the A underneath the B</u> to give "$X = \frac{B}{A}$",
divide, and that's your answer:

$$x = \frac{39}{-15} = -2.6 \qquad \text{So } \underline{x = -2.6}$$

## The Acid Test:
LEARN the <u>6 STEPS</u> for <u>solving equations</u>.
Turn over and write them down.

1) Solve the following equations:   a) $5(x + 2) = 8 + 4(5 - x)$   b) $\dfrac{4}{x + 3} = \dfrac{6}{4 - x}$

# Number Patterns

This is an easy topic, but make sure you know <u>ALL SIX</u> types of sequence, not just the first few. The *main secret* is to *write the differences in the gaps* between each pair of numbers. That way you can usually see what's happening whichever type it is.

## 1) "Common Difference" Type — dead easy

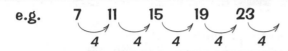

e.g.
```
  7    11    15    19    23          112   105    98    91    84    77
    4     4     4     4     4             7     7     7     7     7
```

## 2) "Increasing Difference" Type

Here the differences <u>increase by the</u> <u>same amount</u> each time:

e.g.
```
  8    11    15    20    26
    3     4     5     6     7
```

## 3) "Decreasing Difference" Type

Here the differences <u>decrease by</u> <u>the same amount</u> each time:

e.g.
```
  53    43    34    26    19    13
     10     9     8     7     6
```

## 4) "Multiplying Factor" Type

This type has a common <u>MULTIPLIER</u> linking each pair of numbers:

e.g.
```
  5    10    20    40
    x2    x2    x2    x2
```

## 5) "Dividing Factor" Type

This type has a common <u>DIVIDER</u> linking each pair of numbers:

e.g.
```
  189   63    21     7
     ÷3    ÷3    ÷3    ÷3
```

## 6) "Adding Previous Terms" Type

Add the *first two terms* to get the *3rd*, then add the *2nd and 3rd* to get the *4th*, etc.

e.g.
```
   1    1    2    3    5    8    13    21
       1+1  1+2  2+3  3+5  5+8  8+13  13+21
```

## The Acid Test:

LEARN the <u>6 types of number pattern</u>. Then cover the page and answer these:

1) Write down <u>FROM MEMORY</u> the name of each type of number sequence and give an example of each.
2) Find the next two terms in these sequences:
   a) 2,6,18,54...    b) 1,3,4,7,11....    c) 3,5,8,12,17,...    d) 128,64,32,...

# Finding the n^th Term

"The n$^{th}$ term" is a formula with "n" in it which gives you every term in a sequence when you put different values for n in.  There are two different types of sequence (for "nth term" questions) which have to be done in different ways:

## Common Difference Type: | "dn + (a − d)"

For any sequence such as  3,  7,  11,  15,  where there's a <u>COMMON DIFFERENCE</u>:

4   4   4

you can always find "the n$^{th}$ term" using the <u>FORMULA</u>:  **n$^{th}$ Term = dn + (a−d)**

<u>Don't forget</u>:

1) "a" is simply the value of <u>THE FIRST TERM</u> in the sequence.
2) "d" is simply the value of <u>THE COMMON DIFFERENCE</u> between the terms.
3) To get the <u>nth term</u>, you just <u>find the values of "a" and "d" from the sequence and stick them in the formula</u>.
   *You don't replace n though — that wants to stay as n*
4) Of course <u>YOU HAVE TO LEARN THE FORMULA</u>, but life is like that.

### Example: | *"Find the n$^{th}$ term of this sequence:   5,   8,   11,   14, ..."*

<u>ANSWER</u>:  1) The formula is dn + (a − d)
2) The <u>first term</u> is 5, so <u>a = 5</u>      The <u>common difference</u> is 3 so <u>d = 3</u>
3) Putting these in the formula gives:        n$^{th}$ term = 3n + (5 − 3)
so <u>n$^{th}$ term = 3n + 2</u>

## Changing Difference Type:

### "a + (n−1)d + ½(n−1)(n−2)C"

If the number sequence is one where the *difference* between the terms is *increasing or decreasing* then it gets a whole lot more complicated (as you'll have spotted from the above formula — which you'll have to *learn!*).  This time there are *THREE* letters you have to fill in:

"a" is the <u>FIRST TERM</u>,
"d" is the <u>FIRST DIFFERENCE</u> (between the first two numbers),
"C" is the <u>CHANGE BETWEEN ONE DIFFERENCE AND THE NEXT</u>.

### Example: | *"Find the n$^{th}$ term of this sequence:   2,   5,   9,   14, ..."*

3   4   5

<u>ANSWER</u>:   1) The formula is   *"a + (n−1)d + ½(n−1)(n−2)C"*
2) The <u>first term</u> is 2, so <u>a = 2</u>      The <u>first difference</u> is 3 so <u>d = 3</u>
3) The <u>differences increase</u> by 1 each time so <u>C = +1</u>
Putting these in the formula gives:     *"2 + (n−1)3 + ½(n−1)(n−2)×1"*
Which becomes:         2 + 3n − 3 + ½n$^2$ − 1½n + 1
Which simplifies to:     ½n$^2$ + 1½n = ½n(n+3)
so the <u>n$^{th}$ term = ½n(n+3)</u>         (Easy peasy, huh!)

## The Acid Test: | LEARN the <u>definition of the n$^{th}$ term</u> and the <u>2 methods for finding it</u>, and LEARN THE FORMULAS.

1) Find the nth term of the following sequences:
a)  4, 7, 10, 13....   b)  3, 8, 13, 18,....   c)  1, 3, 6, 10, 15,....   d)  3, 4, 7, 12,...

# Graphs and (X , Y) Coordinates

## Positive(+) and Negative(−) Coordinates

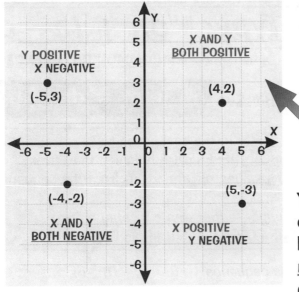

A graph has _four different regions_ where the X- and Y- coordinates are either _positive_ or _negative_.

The easiest region by far is this one because _all the coordinates are positive_.

You have to be dead careful in the other regions though, because one or both of the coordinates will be _negative_, and that always makes life difficult.

## Coordinates — _Getting Them in the Right Order_

Always give <u>COORDINATES IN BRACKETS</u> like this: <u>( X , Y )</u>
And make sure you get them <u>the right way round</u> —

Here are 3 handy rules to help you remember:

1) The two coordinates are always in <u>ALPHABETICAL ORDER, X then Y</u>.

2) **X** is always the flat axis going <u>ACROSS</u> the page. In other words
" <u>X is a..cross</u> "    Get it? — **X** is a "×"        (Hilarious isn't it)

3) You always go <u>IN THE HOUSE</u> (→) and then <u>UP THE STAIRS</u> (↑), so
it's <u>ALONG first</u> and <u>then UP</u>,    i.e. X-coordinate first,  then Y.

## The Acid Test:

1)  Write down the coordinates of all the points A to H.
2)  Plot these points on the graph, join them up, and
name the shape you get:
P(6,-1), Q(0,-6), R(-5,0), S(1,5).

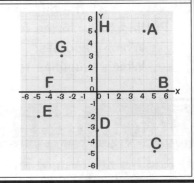

# Regular Polygons

A <u>POLYGON</u> is a <u>MANY-SIDED SHAPE</u>. A <u>REGULAR</u> polygon is one where <u>ALL THE SIDES AND ANGLES ARE THE SAME</u>. The <u>REGULAR POLYGONS</u> are a <u>never-ending</u> series of shapes with some fancy features. <u>They're very easy to learn</u>.

## EQUILATERAL TRIANGLE

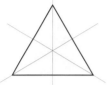

<u>3</u> sides
<u>3 lines</u> of symmetry
Rot<sup>nl</sup> symm. <u>order 3</u>

## SQUARE

<u>4</u> sides
<u>4 lines</u> of symmetry
Rot<sup>nl</sup> symm. <u>order 4</u>

## REGULAR PENTAGON

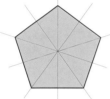

<u>5</u> sides
<u>5 lines</u> of symmetry
Rot<sup>nl</sup> symm. <u>order 5</u>

## REGULAR HEXAGON

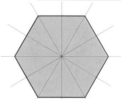

<u>6</u> sides
<u>6 lines</u> of symmetry
Rot<sup>nl</sup> symm. <u>order 6</u>

## REGULAR HEPTAGON

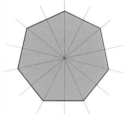

<u>7</u> sides
<u>7 lines</u> of symmetry
Rot<sup>nl</sup> symm. <u>order 7</u>

A 50p piece is like a heptagon

## REGULAR OCTAGON

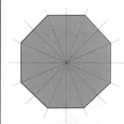

<u>8</u> sides
<u>8 lines</u> of symmetry
Rot<sup>nl</sup> symm. <u>order 8</u>

# Interior And Exterior Angles

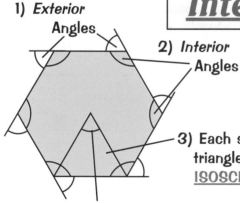

1) *Exterior* Angles

2) *Interior* Angles

3) Each sector triangle is <u>ISOSCELES</u>

4) This angle is always the same as the Exterior Angles

This is the <u>MAIN BUSINESS</u>. Whenever you get a <u>Regular Polygon</u>, it's a <u>cosmic certainty</u> you'll need to work out the <u>Interior and Exterior Angles</u>, because they are the <u>KEY</u> to it all.

$$\text{EXTERIOR ANGLE} = \frac{360°}{\text{No. of Sides}}$$

$$\text{INTERIOR ANGLE} = 180° - \text{EXTERIOR ANGLE}$$

## The Acid Test:

LEARN THIS PAGE.
Then cover it up and answer these little jokers:

1) What is a Regular Polygon?    2) Name the first six of them.
3) Draw a Pentagon and a Hexagon and put in all their lines of symmetry.
4) What are the two important formulas?
5) Work out the two key angles for a Pentagon    6) And for a 12-sided Regular Polygon

# Symmetry

There are <u>THREE TYPES</u> of symmetry. Make sure you know them all:

## 1) Line Symmetry

Where you draw a <u>MIRROR LINE</u> across a picture <u>both sides will fold exactly together</u>.

| 2 LINES OF SYMMETRY | 1 LINE OF SYMMETRY | 1 LINE OF SYMMETRY | 3 LINES OF SYMMETRY | NO LINES OF SYMMETRY | 1 LINE OF SYMMETRY |

### How to draw a reflection:

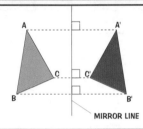

MIRROR LINE

1) Reflect each point one by one

2) Use <u>a line which crosses the mirror line at 90° and goes</u> *EXACTLY the same distance* <u>on the other side of the mirror line</u>, as shown.

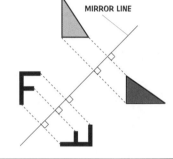

MIRROR LINE

## 2) Plane Symmetry

<u>Plane Symmetry</u> is all to do with <u>3-D SOLIDS</u>. Whereas <u>flat shapes</u> can have a <u>mirror line</u>, <u>solid 3-D objects</u> can have <u>planes of symmetry</u>.

A plane mirror surface can be drawn through many regular solids, but the shape must be <u>EXACTLY THE SAME ON BOTH SIDES OF THE PLANE</u> (i.e. mirror images), like these are:

Planes of Symmetry

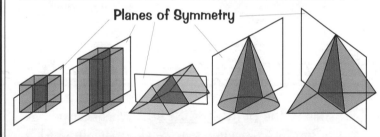

The shapes drawn here all have <u>MANY MORE PLANES OF SYMMETRY</u> but there's only one drawn in for each shape, because otherwise it would all get really messy and you wouldn't be able to see anything.

## 3) Rotational Symmetry

This is where you can <u>ROTATE</u> the shape into different positions that <u>all look exactly the same</u>.

| Order 1 | Order 2 | Order 2 | Order 3 | Order 4 |

1) The <u>ORDER OF ROTATIONAL SYMMETRY</u> is the fancy way of saying: <u>"HOW MANY DIFFERENT POSITIONS LOOK THE SAME"</u>.

e.g. you should say the Z shape above has "Rotational symmetry order 2"

2) BUT... when a shape has <u>ONLY 1 POSITION</u> you can <u>EITHER</u> say that it has "Rotational Symmetry order 1" OR that it has "NO Rotational Symmetry".

# Transformations

It's easy to throw away marks in the exam by not giving enough information.
Always make sure you specify _all the details_ for each transformation.

## 1) TRANSLATION

> You must specify this ONE detail:
>
> 1) The **VECTOR OF TRANSLATION** $\left(\begin{smallmatrix} x \to \\ \uparrow y \end{smallmatrix}\right)$ (See P.83 on vector notation)

All that changes in a translation is the _POSITION_ of the object — _everything else_ remains _unchanged_.

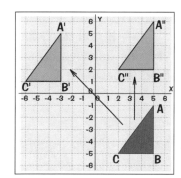

ABC to A'B'C' is a _translation of_ $\begin{pmatrix} -8 \\ 6 \end{pmatrix}$

ABC to A"B"C" is a _translation of_ $\begin{pmatrix} 0 \\ 7 \end{pmatrix}$

## 2) ROTATION

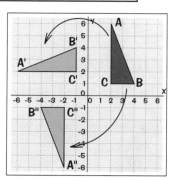

ABC to A'B'C' is a Rotation of <u>90°</u>, <u>anticlockwise</u>, <u>ABOUT the origin</u>.

ABC to A"B"C" is a Rotation of <u>half a turn (180°)</u>, <u>clockwise</u>, <u>ABOUT the origin</u>.

> You must specify these THREE details:
>
> 1) **ANGLE** turned
> 2) **DIRECTION** (Clockwise or..)
> 3) **CENTRE** of Rotation

The only things that _change_ in a rotation are the _POSITION_ and the _ORIENTATION_ of the object. _Everything else_ remains _unchanged_.

## 3) REFLECTION

> You must Specify this ONE detail:
>
> 1) The **MIRROR LINE**

With reflection, the _POSITION_ and _ORIENTATION_ of the object are the _only things that change_.

A to B is a <u>reflection IN the Y-axis</u>.

A to C is a <u>reflection IN the line Y=X</u>

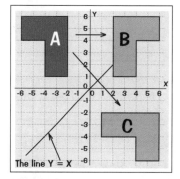

The line Y = X

## The Acid Test:

LEARN _the names of these three transformations and the details that go with each. When you think you know it, turn over and write it all down._

1) Describe _fully_ these transformations:

A − B, B − C, C − A, A − D.

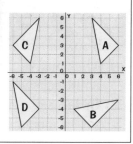

# Combinations of Transformations

In Exam questions they'll often do something _horrid_ like _stick two transformations together_ and then ask you what combination gets you from shape A to shape B.    Be _ready_.

## The Better You Know Them All — The Easier it is

These kinds of question aren't so bad — but _ONLY_ if you've _LEARNT_ the _three transformations_ on the last page _really well_ — if you don't know them, then you certainly won't do too well at spotting a _combination_ of one followed by another.
That's because the method is basically _"Try it and see..."_

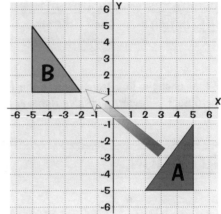

## Example

_"What combination of two transformations takes you from triangle A to triangle B?"_

(There's usually a few different ways of getting from one shape to the other — but remember you only need to find _ONE_ of them.)

## Method: Try an obvious transformation first, and See...

If you _think_ about it, the answer can _only_ be a combination of two of the _three types_ shown on the last page, so you can immediately start to _narrow it down_:

1) First, _try a reflection_ (in either the X-axis or the Y-axis).
   Here we've tried a reflection in the _Y-axis_, to give shape A':

2) You should now easily be able to see the _final step_ from A' to B
   — it's a _translation_ of $\binom{0}{6}$.

And that's it _DONE_ — from A to B is simply a combination of:

> A _REFLECTION IN THE Y-AXIS_ followed by a _TRANSLATION OF_ $\binom{0}{6}$

_At least that's one answer anyway. If instead we decided to reflect it in the X-axis first (as shown here) then we'd get another answer (see Acid Test below) — but both are right._

### "But which transformation do I try first?" I hear you cry.

Well it just depends on _how it looks_.
But the _more transformation questions_ you do, the more obvious that first guess becomes.
In other words: the more you _practise_, the _easier_ you'll be able to do it — surprise surprise...

## The Acid Test:   LEARN the main points on this page. Then cover it up and write them all down.

1) What pair of transformations will convert shape C into shape D?:
   What pair will convert shape D to shape C?
2) In the example above, find the other transformation needed to
   get to shape B after reflecting shape A in the X-axis.

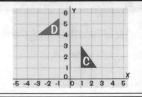

# The Shapes You Need to Know

## These are easy marks in the Exam — make sure you know them all.

**1) SQUARE** (4 <u>equal</u> sides. <u>Opposite</u> sides <u>parallel</u>. 4 equal <u>interior angles of 90°</u>.)

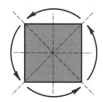

<u>4 lines</u> of symmetry.
Rotational symmetry <u>order 4</u>.

**2) RECTANGLE** (<u>2 pairs</u> of <u>equal</u> sides. <u>Opposite</u> sides <u>parallel</u>. 4 equal <u>interior angles of 90°</u>.)

(one that isn't a square)

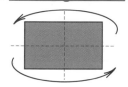

<u>2 lines</u> of symmetry.
Rotational symmetry <u>order 2</u>.

**3) RHOMBUS** (4 <u>equal</u> sides. <u>Opposite</u> sides <u>parallel</u>. <u>Opposite interior angles equal</u>.)

(It's also a diamond)

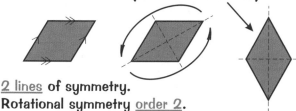

<u>2 lines</u> of symmetry.
Rotational symmetry <u>order 2</u>.

**4) PARALLELOGRAM** (<u>2 pairs</u> of <u>equal</u> sides. <u>Opposite</u> sides <u>parallel</u>. <u>Opposite interior angles equal</u>.)

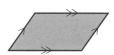
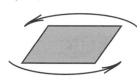

<u>NO lines</u> of symmetry.
Rotational symmetry <u>order 2</u>.

**5) TRAPEZIUM** (<u>1 pair</u> of <u>parallel sides</u>.)

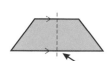

Only the <u>isosceles trapezium</u> has a <u>line</u> of symmetry.
None have rotational symmetry.

**6) KITE**

(<u>2 pairs</u> of <u>equal</u> sides. <u>1 pair</u> of <u>equal interior angles</u>.)

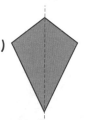

<u>1 line</u> of symmetry.
No rotational symmetry.

**7) EQUILATERAL <u>Triangle</u>**

(<u>3 equal sides</u>.)

<u>3 lines</u> of symmetry.
Rotational symmetry <u>order 3</u>.

**8) <u>RIGHT-ANGLED</u> <u>Triangle</u>**

No symmetry unless the angles are <u>45°</u>.

**9) <u>ISOSCELES</u> <u>Triangle</u>**

(2 sides equal 2 angles equal.)

<u>1 line</u> of symmetry.
No rotational symmetry.

**10) <u>SOLIDS</u>**

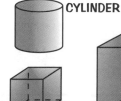

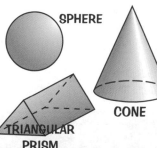
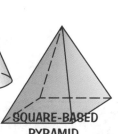

REGULAR TETRAHEDRON
CYLINDER
SPHERE
CUBE
CUBOID
TRIANGULAR PRISM
CONE
SQUARE-BASED PYRAMID

# The Acid Test: LEARN <u>everything on this page</u>.

Then turn over and write down all the details that you can remember. Then try again.

# Circles

## 1) π "A Number a Bit Bigger than 3"

The big thing to remember is that π (called "pi") only seems confusing because it's a scary-looking Greek letter. In the end, it's just an _ordinary number_ (3.14159...) _which is rounded off to either 3 or 3.14 or 3.142_ (depending on how accurate you want to be).
And that's all it is:  _A NUMBER A BIT BIGGER THAN 3_.

## 2) Diameter is TWICE the Radius

The _DIAMETER_ goes right across the circle.
_EXAMPLES:_  The _RADIUS_ only goes _halfway_ across.

| | |
|---|---|
| If the radius is 4cm, the diameter is 8cm, | If D = 12cm, then r = 6cm, |
| If the radius is 12m, the diameter is 24m, | If diameter = 2mm, then radius = 1mm |

## 3) Use the Diameter to Calculate the Circumference

> **Circumference = π × Diameter**  OR  **C = π × D**

_REMEMBER_: it makes _no difference at all_ whether the question gives you _the radius_ or _the diameter_, because it's dead easy to work out one from the other.

_EXAMPLE:_ "Find the circumference of the circle shown below."

_ANSWER:_  Radius = 5 cm, so _Diameter = 10 cm_ (easy)
C = π × D,  so
C = 3.14 × 10
= _31.4 cm_

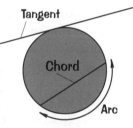

## 4) Arc, Chord and Tangent

A TANGENT is a straight line that _just touches_ the _outside_ of the circle.

A CHORD is a line drawn _across the inside_ of a circle.

AN ARC is just _part of the circumference_ of the circle.

## 5) Sectors and Segments are both Areas

### 5a) SECTOR of a circle

Major Arc   Minor Arc
q  Minor Sector
Major Sector

### 5b) SEGMENT of a circle

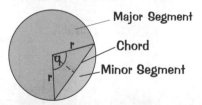

Major Segment
Chord
Minor Segment

## The Acid Test:

There are _5 SECTIONS_ on this page.
They're all _mighty important_ — LEARN THEM.

Now cover the page and _write down_ everything you've learnt. Frightening isn't it.
1) A plate has a diameter of 14cm. Find the circumference of it using the methods you've just learnt. Remember to show all your working out.

# <u>Geometry</u>

## <u>8 Simple Rules</u> — <u>that's all</u>:

<u>If you know them ALL — THOROUGHLY</u>, you at least have a fighting chance of working out problems with lines and angles. *If you don't — you've no chance*.

### 1) <u>Angles in a</u> <u>Triangle</u>

Add up to <u>180°</u>.

$$a+b+c=180°$$

### 2) <u>Angles on a</u> <u>Straight Line</u>

Add up to <u>180°</u>.

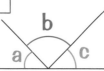

$$a+b+c=180°$$

### 3) <u>Angles in a</u> <u>4-sided Shape</u>

(a <u>"Quadrilateral"</u>)

Add up to <u>360°</u>.

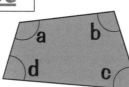

$$a+b+c+d=360°$$

### 4) <u>Angles</u> <u>round a Point</u>

Add up to <u>360°</u>.

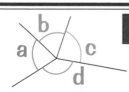

$$a+b+c+d=360°$$

### 5) <u>Exterior Angle</u> <u>of</u> <u>Triangle</u>

Exterior Angle of triangle
= sum of Opposite Interior angles

i.e. $a+b=d$

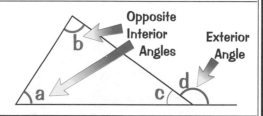

Opposite Interior Angles

Exterior Angle

### 6) <u>Equilateral, Isosceles</u> <u>and</u> <u>Right-angled</u> <u>Triangles</u>

These three triangles have special angle properties. <u>Learn them</u>.

**6a) <u>EQUILATERAL</u>**

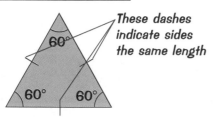

*These dashes indicate sides the same length*

<u>3 sides equal.</u>
<u>3 internal angles equal to 60°.</u>

**6b) <u>ISOSCELES</u>**

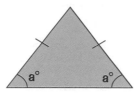

<u>2 sides equal.</u>
<u>2 internal angles equal.</u>

**6c) <u>RIGHT-ANGLED</u>**

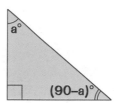

$(90-a)°$

<u>1 internal angle of 90°.</u>
<u>Other 2 internal angles add up to 90°.</u>

# *Geometry*

## 7) *Parallel lines*

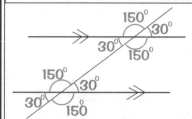

Whenever one line goes across
2 parallel lines, then <u>the two
bunches of angles are the same</u>
(The arrows mean those 2 lines are
parallel)

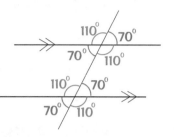

> Whenever you have <u>TWO PARALLEL LINES</u> there are *only two different angles*:
> <u>A SMALL ONE</u> and <u>A BIG ONE</u> and they <u>ALWAYS ADD UP TO 180°</u>.
> E.g.   30° and 150°  or  70° and 110°

The trickiest bit about parallel lines is <u>spotting them in the first place</u>
— watch out for these "Z", "C", "U" and "F" shapes popping up:

SAME

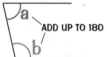
ADD UP TO 180

ADD UP TO 180

SAME

In a <u>Z-shape</u> they're called
"<u>ALTERNATE ANGLES</u>"

If they add up to 180 they're called
"<u>SUPPLEMENTARY ANGLES</u>"

In an F-shape they're called
"<u>CORRESPONDING ANGLES</u>"

**Alas you're expected to learn these three silly names too!**

Try using this stuff to work out the angle properties of a parallelogram.

If necessary, <u>EXTEND
THE LINES</u> to make
the diagram <u>easier to
get to grips with</u>:

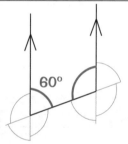
60°

## 8) *Irregular Polygons:   Interior and Exterior Angles*

An irregular polygon is basically any shape with lots of straight sides which aren't all the
same.  There are two formulas you need to know:

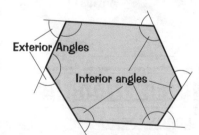
Exterior Angles
Interior angles

> <u>Sum of Exterior angles = 360°</u>

> <u>Sum of Interior angles = (n − 2)×180°</u>
> where n is the number of sides

The (n − 2)×180° formula comes from splitting the inside of the
polygon up into triangles using full diagonals.  Each triangle has
180° in it so just count up the triangles and times by 180°.  There's
always 2 less triangles than there are sides, hence the (n − 2).

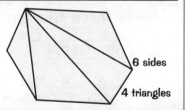
6 sides
4 triangles

## *The Acid Test:*

LEARN EVERYTHING on these two pages.  Then <u>turn
over</u> and see how much of it you can <u>write down</u>.

1) Find the size of angle Z in the triangle shown:
2) How much do the exterior angles of a 7-sided polygon add up to?
3) How much do the interior angles of a 5-sided polygon add up to?
4) One of the diagrams above has one angle given as 60°.  Find the other 7 angles.

50°
z

# Bearings

## Bearings — 3 Key Points

N  The bearing of A from B

A

B

1) A bearing is the **DIRECTION TRAVELLED** between two points, **GIVEN AS AN ANGLE** in degrees.

2) All bearings are measured **CLOCKWISE** from the **NORTHLINE**.

3) All bearings should be given as **3 figures**, e.g. 243°, 060° (not 60°), 008° (not 8°), 018° etc.

## The 3 Key Words

Only learn this if you want to get bearings *RIGHT*

### 1) "FROM"

*Find the word "FROM" in the question,* and put your pencil on the diagram at the point you are going "*from*".

### 2) NORTHLINE

At the point you are going "FROM", *draw in a NORTHLINE.*

### 3) CLOCKWISE

Now draw in the angle CLOCKWISE *from the northline to the line joining the two points*. This angle is the **BEARING**.

## Example

Find the bearing of Q from P:

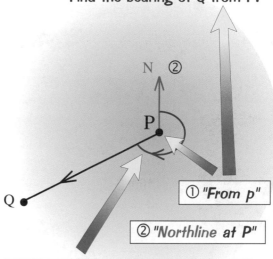

N  ②

P

Q

① "From p"

② "Northline at P"

③ *"Clockwise, from the N-line".*

This angle is the *bearing of Q from P* and is *245°*.

## The Acid Test:

LEARN the 3 Features of Bearings and the 3 Key Steps of the method for finding them.

Now turn over and write down what you've just learnt.
Keep trying till you can write down all six points from memory.

1) Find the bearing of H from T.  (Use a protractor)
2) Find the bearing of T from H.

T

H

# Conversion Factors

Conversion Factors are a very powerful tool for dealing with a wide variety of questions — and the method is very easy.

## Method

1) Find the <u>Conversion Factor</u>  (always easy)

2) <u>Multiply by it AND divide by it</u>

3) Choose the <u>common sense answer</u>

## Three Important *Examples*

**1)**  *"Convert 2.55 hours into minutes."*   (This is NOT 2hrs 55mins)

1) Conversion factor = <u>60</u>          — (simply because 1 hour = <u>60</u> mins )
2) 2.55 hrs × 60 = 153 mins (makes sense)
   2.55 hrs ÷ 60 = 0.0425 mins (ridiculous answer!)
3) So plainly the answer is that  2.55hrs = <u>153 mins</u>     (=2hrs 33mins)

**2)**  *"If £1 = 7.75 French Francs, how much is 47.36 Francs in £ and p?"*

1) Obviously, Conversion Factor = <u>7.75</u>   (The "exchange rate")
2) 47.36 × 7.75 = £367.04
   47.36 ÷ 7.75 = £6.11
3) Not quite so obvious this time, but if roughly 8 Francs = £1, then 47 Francs can't be much — certainly not £367, so the answer must be <u>£6.11p</u>

**3)**  *"A map has a scale of 1:20,000. How big in real life is a distance of 3cm on the map?"*

1) Conversion Factor = 20 000
2) 3cm × 20 000 = 60 000cm  (looks OK)
   3cm ÷ 20 000 = 0.00015cm  (not good)
3) So 60,000cm is the answer.
   How do we convert to metres?

To Convert 60,000cm to m:

1) C.F. = 100    (cm ←− m)
2) 60,000 × 100 = 6,000,000m  (hmm)
   60,000 ÷ 100 = <u>600m</u>  (more like it)
3) So answer = <u>600m</u>

## The Acid Test:

LEARN the <u>3 steps</u> of the <u>Conversion Factor</u> method. Then turn over and <u>write them down.</u>

1) Convert **2.3 km** into metres.
2) Which is more, **£34** or **260 French Francs**?  (Use 7.75)
3) A map is drawn to a scale of **2cm = 5km**.  A road is **8 km** long.  How many cm will this be on the map?  (Hint, C.F. = 5÷2, i.e. 1 cm = 2.5 km)

# Frequency Tables and Bar Charts

## Is the Data Discrete or Continuous?

There are 2 different data types that you'll have to deal with in the exam:

Discrete — This is data that takes definite values and can be recorded exactly, e.g. number of books on a table (i.e. you could have 1 book or 2 books, but not 1.73 books).

Continuous — This is data which can only be recorded to a limited level of accuracy, and can take ANY value in a range, e.g. heights of people in a year group. Data like this has to be grouped, e.g. "number of people with heights between 140cm and 150cm".

## What Does "40 ≤ w < 50" Mean?

It basically means the value of w is between 40 and 50. But.... you also need to know:
    1) the ≤ symbol means w can be EQUAL TO 40   (or greater than 40)
    2) the < symbol means w must be LESS THAN 50   (to go in this group)
The upshot of all this is that a value of 40 will go in this group: $40 \leq w < 50$,
whereas a value of 50 will have to go in the next group up: $50 \leq w < 60$.

## An Important Example

The weights (in kg) of a bunch of 30 school kids are shown below. The tally table and bar chart have been done. You'll notice each number was crossed off as it was done:

67, 45, 47, 65, 54, 76, 44, 34, 69, 53, 32, 54, 78, 59, 57,
30, 79, 46, 66, 51, 40, 53, 35, 47, 59, 60, 64, 45, 49, 50

| Weight $w$ (kg) | Tally | Frequency |
|---|---|---|
| $30 \leq w < 40$ | IIII | 4 |
| $40 \leq w < 50$ | HHT III | 8 |
| $50 \leq w < 60$ | HHT IIII | 9 |
| $60 \leq w < 70$ | HHT I | 6 |
| $70 \leq w < 80$ | III | 3 |

Once you've done a frequency table the next thing is to draw a bar chart.

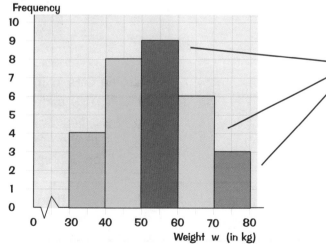

These numbers here are ALWAYS just THE HEIGHTS OF THE BARS in the bar chart.

E.g. there are 9 people between 50 and 60 kg, so the bar drawn between 50 and 60 goes up to 9.

# Tables, Charts and Graphs

## 1) Two-Way Tables

Two-way tables are a bit like frequency tables, but they show <u>two</u> things instead of just <u>one</u>.

### EXAMPLE:

*"Use this table to work out how many*
*(a) right-handed people and*
*(b) left-handed women there were in this survey."*

|  | Women | Men | TOTAL |
|---|---|---|---|
| Left-handed |  | 27 | 63 |
| Right-handed | 164 | 173 |  |
| TOTAL | 200 | 200 | 400 |

### ANSWER:

(a) Either: (i) <u>add up</u> the number of right-handed women and the number of right-handed men. So that's 164 + 173 = <u>*337 right-handed people*</u>.

Or: (ii) <u>take away</u> the total number of left-handed people from the total number of people. So that's 400 – 63 = <u>*337 right-handed people*</u>.

(b) Either: (i) take away the number of right-handed women from the total number of women. That's 200 – 164 = <u>*36 left-handed women*</u>.

Or: (ii) take away the left-handed men from the total number of left-handed people. Which would be 63 – 27 = <u>*36 left-handed women*</u>.

## 2) Pictograms

— these use <u>pictures</u> instead of <u>numbers</u>.

EXAMPLE: The *pictogram* opposite shows the number of talking cats used in ridiculous TV adverts in a 3-month period: 🐱 = 500 talking cats.

| May | 🐱 🐱 🐱 | (1500 ridiculous talking cats) |
| June | 🐱 🐱 ▪ | (1250 ridiculous talking cats) |
| July | 🐱 🐱 🐱 🐱 | (2000 ridiculous talking cats) |

In a PICTOGRAM each picture or symbol represents a certain number of items.

## 3) Bar Charts

Just watch out for when the bars should touch or not touch:

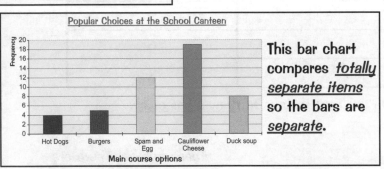

Popular Choices at the School Canteen

This bar chart compares <u>*totally separate items*</u> so the bars are <u>*separate*</u>.

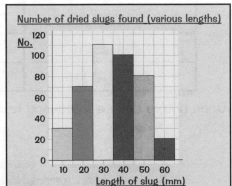

Number of dried slugs found (various lengths)

ALL the bars in this chart are for LENGTHS and you must <u>*put every possible length into one bar or the next*</u> so there mustn't be any spaces.

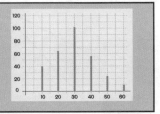

A <u>BAR-LINE GRAPH</u> is just like a bar chart except you draw thin lines instead of bars.

## The Acid Test:

Learn all three sections on this page. Then copy out the two-way table, turn over the page and fill in the blanks.

# More on Bar Charts and Sample Sizes

## The Bar Chart's Shape shows the "Spread" of Data

You must **LEARN the TWO SHAPES** of bar charts:

### 1) A Nice Smooth, Shallow Curve

This one shows a _large spread_ of results _away from the middle_.
(E.g. the weights of a sample of 16 year olds will cover a wide range.)

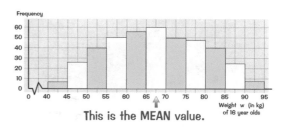

This is the MEAN value.

### 2) Rising Steeply to a Point in the Middle

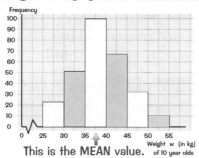

This is the MEAN value.

This shape shows a _small spread_ of results away from the middle — _most of the results are within a narrow range_.
(E.g. the weights of a sample of 10 year olds will have a narrow range.)

## Bigger Sample Sizes give Better Results

If you're doing a survey, you select a _sample_ of people to ask. The _bigger_ the sample (ie the _more people you ask_), the _better your results_ will be.

There are four different ways of choosing a sample of people:

1) Pick people "_at random_".

2) Pick out, say, _every 10$^{th}$ or 100$^{th}$_ one (e.g. giving every 10$^{th}$ customer a questionnaire)

3) Where there's different 'layers' to choose from — classes/pupils; departments/ employees etc. — and you pick _a few from each different group_.

4) Pick a group of people that's _representative of the population_ (e.g. same ratio of males to females, adults to children, etc.).

Main thing to remember is this:

> FOR _ANY_ SURVEY, THE _BIGGER_ THE _SAMPLE SIZE_
> (i.e. the more people asked), THE _BETTER REPRESENTATION_
> YOU'LL GET OF THE _WHOLE POPULATION_.

## The Acid Test:

Learn the two shapes of bar charts. Then close the book, sketch them and jot down the details about each.

# Probability

Probability definitely seems a bit of a "Black Art" to most people. It's not as bad as you think, but YOU MUST LEARN THE BASIC FACTS, which is what we have on the next two pages.

## 1) All Probabilities are between 0 and 1

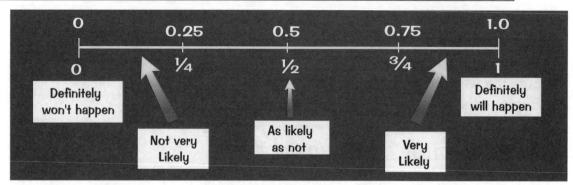

Probabilities can only have values between 0 and 1, and you should be able to put the probability of any event happening on this scale of 0 to 1.

You can give probabilities using either:     FRACTIONS, DECIMALS or PERCENTAGES.

## 2) Equal Probabilities

When the different results all have the same chance of happening, then the probabilities will be EQUAL. These are the two cases which usually come up in Exams:

1) TOSSING A COIN:     Equal chance of getting a head or a tail (½)

2) THROWING A DICE:     Equal chance of getting any of the numbers ($\frac{1}{6}$)

## 3) Unequal Probabilities You Can Work Out

These make for more interesting questions.
(Which means you'll get them in the Exam.)

**EXAMPLE:**     "A bag contains 6 blue balls, 5 red balls and 9 green balls. Find the probability of picking out a green ball."

**ANSWER:**

The chances of picking out the three colours are NOT EQUAL.

The probability of picking a green is simply:

$$\frac{\text{NUMBER OF GREENS}}{\text{TOTAL NUMBER OF BALLS}} = \frac{9}{20}$$

# Probability

## 4) Unequal Probabilities You'd Need to Test

In many real-life situations the probabilities are not equal, like in these examples:

1) The probabilities of either winning, drawing or losing a game (not 1/3 each!)
2) The chance that the next car to pass will be red or blue or white etc.
3) A BIASED DICE coming up with a "six" compared to any other number.
4) The chance of passing or failing a test.

In all these cases you can only find the probabilities by doing A TEST OR A SURVEY
— they might ask you to say just that in the Exam to see if you know it.

## 5) The Probability of the OPPOSITE Happening is just the rest of the probability that's left over

This is simple enough AS LONG AS YOU REMEMBER IT.
If the probability of something happening is 0.3 then the chance of it NOT HAPPENING is just the rest of the probability that's left over — in this case, 0.7 (so that it adds up to 1).

Example:     A loaded dice has a 0.25 chance of coming up TWO.
             What is the chance of it *not* coming up TWO?
Answer:      1 – 0.25 = 0.75
             So, the chance of the dice *not* coming up TWO is 0.75

## 6) Listing All Outcomes: 2 Coins, Dice, Spinners

A simple question you might get is to list all the possible results from tossing two coins or two spinners or a dice and a spinner, etc. Whatever it is, it'll be very similar to these, so LEARN THEM:

The *possible outcomes* from
TOSSING TWO COINS are:

| | | |
|---|---|---|
| Head | Head | H H |
| Head | Tail | H T |
| Tail | Head | T H |
| Tail | Tail | T T |

From TWO SPINNERS with 3 sides:

| | | |
|---|---|---|
| BLUE + 1 | RED + 1 | GREEN + 1 |
| BLUE + 2 | RED + 2 | GREEN + 2 |
| BLUE + 3 | RED + 3 | GREEN + 3 |

Try and list the possible outcomes METHODICALLY
— to make sure you get them ALL.

## The Acid Test

1) If a bag contains 12 red balls, 5 green balls and 4 blue balls, what's the probability that a red one is picked? What's the chance that a white one is picked?
2) A biased dice is made so that the chance of getting a SIX is 0.22. What is the chance of NOT GETTING A SIX?
3) List ALL THE POSSIBLE OUTCOMES when a coin and a dice are thrown together.

# Revision Test for Stage One

These questions may seem difficult, *but they're the very best revision you can do*. The whole point of revision, remember, is to find out what you *don't* know and then learn it until you do. These searching questions *really* test how much you know. The questions are in page order, so you can easily look up anything you don't know.

## Keep learning these basic facts until you know them

1) What are the 2 rules for rounding whole numbers?

2) Write down the rule for multiplying and dividing with negative numbers.

3) Write down the two-step method for finding prime numbers (below 120).

4) What is the best method for finding all the factors of a number?

5) What are the prime factors of a number? How do you find them?

6) Explain exactly what HCF and LCM mean.

7) List the first ten terms in each of these sequences:
   a) even numbers  b) odd numbers   c) square numbers       d) cube numbers
   e) powers of 2     f) powers of 10    g) triangle numbers

8) Explain what the square root and cube root of a number are.

9) State the rules for multiplying and dividing by factors of ten.

10) Give an example of a fraction that gives a terminating decimal, and one that doesn't.

11) Describe in words the 6 rules for doing fractions by hand.

12) Which is the fraction button on your calculator? What must you press to enter $2\frac{3}{4}$?

13) Describe the 3 types of percentage question, say how to identify each and give details of the methods for solving them.

14) Write down the formula for percentage change, and give 3 examples of it.

15) Which is the powers button on your calculator? What must you press to find $8^{15}$?

16) Which are the memory buttons on your calculator? What are they used for?

17) What does BODMAS mean and what has it got to do with your calculator?

18) Write a formula for the total cost, **C**, of buying **n** bat wings at **X** pence each, and **m** lizard tongues at **Y** pence each.

19) Calculate **C** from the previous question if $n = 4$, $m = 7$, $X = 26$ and $Y = 18$.

20) In algebra, what is a:  a) term?   b) expression?   c) equation?   d) identity?

21) Write out the method for factorising an expression. Factorise: $12x^3y^4 + 4x^2y^3z - 8xy^3$

22) Describe the commutative, associative and distributive laws.

23) Explain the "common sense" and "trial and error" methods of solving equations.

24) List the 6 steps of the formal method for solving equations.

25) Name the 6 different types of number pattern and give an example of each.

26) Write down the formula for finding the $n^{th}$ term of a "changing difference" number pattern.

27) What is a regular polygon? Draw the first 6, and describe their symmetry.

28) What are the 3 types of symmetry? Draw an example for each.

29) Describe the 3 main transformations as fully as you can.

30) Draw and name 6 different quadrilaterals. Describe their geometrical properties and symmetry.

31) Write down the formula for the circumference of a circle. What is $\pi$?

32) Draw a circle and mark on it: radius, diameter, arc, chord, tangent, sector and segment.

33) List 8 rules of geometry.

34) Write down the 3 key words for bearings, and explain their importance.

35) State the 3 steps of the method for applying conversion factors.

36) In a frequency table, what does $50 \leq x < 60$ mean?

37) What are the 4 different ways of choosing a sample of people for a survey?

38) If the probability of something happening is **x**, what is the probability of it **not** happening?

# Rounding Off

There are _two different ways_ of specifying _where_ a number should be _rounded off_.
They are: "Decimal Places" and "Significant Figures". Doing "Decimal Places" is easier.

## Decimal Places  (d.p.)

**1) Identify the position of the LAST DIGIT.**

**2) Then look at the next digit to the RIGHT — called the DECIDER.**

**3) If the DECIDER is 5 or more, then ROUND-UP the LAST DIGIT.
If the DECIDER is 4 or less, then leave the LAST DIGIT as it is.**

This is pretty easy:

1) To round off to, say, 4 decimal places, the _LAST DIGIT_ will be
the _4th one after the decimal point_.

2) There must be _no more digits_ after the LAST DIGIT (not even zeros).

## Significant Figures  (Sig. Fig.)

The method for sig. fig. is _identical_ to that for d.p. except that finding the _position_ of the _LAST DIGIT_ is more difficult — it wouldn't be so bad, but for the ZEROS ...

**1) The 1st significant figure of any number is simply
THE FIRST DIGIT WHICH ISN'T A ZERO.**

**2) The 2nd, 3rd, 4th, etc. significant figures follow on immediately
after the 1st, REGARDLESS OF BEING ZEROS OR NOT ZEROS.**

e.g      0.002309                    2.03070

_SIG FIGS:_   1st 2nd 3rd 4th         1st 2nd 3rd  4th

(If we're rounding to say, 3 sig. fig. then the LAST DIGIT is simply the 3rd sig. fig.)

**3) After _Rounding Off_ the LAST DIGIT, end ZEROS must be filled in
up to, BUT NOT BEYOND, the decimal point.**

No _extra zeros_ must ever be put in _after_ the decimal point.

| Examples | to 4 s.f. | to 3 s.f. | to 2 s.f. | to 1 s.f. |
|---|---|---|---|---|
| 1) 17.0067 | 17.01 | 17.0 | 17 | 20 |
| 2) 0.0045902 | 0.004590 | 0.00459 | 0.0046 | 0.005 |
| 3) 30895.4 | 30900 | 30900 | 31000 | 30000 |

## The Acid Test:
**LEARN the whole of this page, then turn over and write down everything you've learned.** It's all good clean fun.

1) Round 3.5743 to 2 decimal places       2) Give 0.0481 to 2 decimal places
3) Express 12.9096 to 3 d.p.       4) Express 3546.054 to 1 d.p.
5) Round these to 3 s.f. _and for each one_ say which of the 3 rules about ZEROS applies:
   a) 567.78   b) 23445   c) 0.04563   d) 0.90876

# Accuracy and Estimating

## Appropriate Accuracy

In the Exam you may well get a question asking for "an appropriate degree of accuracy" for a certain measurement.

So how do you decide what is *appropriate accuracy*? The key to this is *the number of significant figures* (See P.41) that you give it to, and these are the simple rules:

### 1) For fairly casual measurements, 2 SIGNIFICANT FIGURES is most appropriate.

EXAMPLES:
  COOKING — 250 g (2 sig. fig.) of sugar,
            (*not* 253 g (3 S.F.), or 300 g (1 s.f.))
  DISTANCE OF A JOURNEY — 450 miles or 25 miles or 3500 miles (All 2 s.f.)
  AREA OF A GARDEN OR FLOOR — 330 m² or 15 m²

### 2) For MORE IMPORTANT OR TECHNICAL THINGS, 3 SIGNIFICANT FIGURES is essential.

EXAMPLES:
  A LENGTH that will be CUT TO FIT, e.g. You'd measure a shelf as 25.6 cm long
            (*not 26 cm or 25.63 cm*)
  A TECHNICAL FIGURE, e.g. 34.2 miles per gallon,
            (*rather than 34 mpg*)
  Any ACCURATE measurement with a ruler: e.g. 67.5 cm, (*not 70 cm or 67.54 cm*)

### 3) Only for REALLY SCIENTIFIC WORK would you have more than 3 SIG FIG.

For example, only someone *really keen* would want to know the length of a piece of string *to the nearest tenth of a mm* — like 34.46 cm, for example.     (*Get a life!*)

## Estimating Calculations

As long as you realise what's expected, this is *VERY EASY*.  People get confused because they *over-complicate it*.   To *estimate* something this is all you do:

**1) ROUND EVERYTHING OFF to nice easy CONVENIENT NUMBERS.**
**2) Then WORK OUT THE ANSWER using those nice easy numbers — and that's it!**

You don't worry about the answer being "wrong", because you're only trying to get a rough idea of the size of the proper answer, e.g. is it about 20 or about 200?

This is a great way of checking your answers, especially if you have to work something out on a calculator. It's easy to tell if you've pressed the wrong button somewhere.

Don't forget though, in the Exam you'll need to *show all the steps you've done*, to prove you didn't just use a calculator.

**Example:** Q: ESTIMATE the value of $\frac{127.8 + 41.9}{56.5 \times 3.2}$ *showing all your working.*

ANSWER:
$$\frac{127.8 + 41.9}{56.5 \times 3.2} \approx \frac{130 + 40}{60 \times 3} \approx \frac{170}{180} \approx 1$$  ( "≈" means *"roughly equal to"* )

# Standard Index Form

Standard Form and Standard Index Form are the SAME THING.
So remember both of these names as well as what it actually is:

Ordinary Number: 4,300,000        In Standard Form:        $4.3 \times 10^6$

Standard form is only really useful for writing VERY BIG or VERY SMALL numbers in a more convenient way, e.g.

56,000,000,000  would  be  $5.6 \times 10^{10}$ in standard form.
0.000 000 003 45 would be $3.45 \times 10^{-9}$ in standard form.

but ANY NUMBER can be written in standard form and you need to know how to do it:

## What it Actually is:

A number written in standard form must ALWAYS be in EXACTLY this form:

$$A \times 10^n$$

This *number* must *always* be BETWEEN 1 AND 10.

(The fancy way of saying this is:

$"1 \leqslant A < 10"$ — they sometimes write that in Exam questions — don't let it put you off, just remember what it means).

This number is just the NUMBER OF PLACES the decimal point moves.

## Learn The Three Rules:

1) The front number must always be BETWEEN 1 AND 10

2) The power of 10, n, is purely: HOW FAR THE D.P. MOVES

3) n is +ve for BIG numbers,    n is –ve for SMALL numbers

(This is much better than rules based on which way the d.p. moves.)

## Examples:

1) "*Express 35 600 in standard form*".

**METHOD:**
1) Move the d.p. until 35 600 becomes 3.56 ("$1 \leqslant A < 10$")
2) The d.p. has moved 4 places so n=4, giving: $10^4$
3) 35600 is a BIG number so n is +4, not –4

ANSWER:
$3.5600.= \underline{3.56 \times 10^4}$

2) "*Express 8.14 x $10^{-3}$ as an ordinary number*".

**METHOD:**
1) $10^{-3}$, tells us that the d.p. must move 3 places...
2) ...and the "–" sign tells us to move the d.p. to make it a SMALL number. (i.e. 0.00814, rather than 8140)

ANSWER:
$8.14 = \underline{0.00814}$

# Standard Index Form

## Standard Form and the Calculator

People usually manage all that stuff about moving the decimal point OK *(apart from always forgetting that FOR A BIG NUMBER it's "ten to the power +ve something" and FOR A SMALL NUMBER it's "ten to the power –ve something")*, but when it comes to doing standard form on a calculator it's invariably a sorry saga of confusion and ineptitude.
But it's not so bad really — you just have to learn it, that's all.....

## 1) Entering Standard Form Numbers EXP

The button you MUST USE to put standard form numbers into the calculator is the EXP

(or EE) button — but DON'T go pressing X 10 as well, like a lot of people do, because that makes it WRONG

### Example: *"Enter 2.67 × 10$^{15}$ into the calculator"*

Just press: 2.67 EXP 15 = and the display will be | 2.67 $^{15}$ |

Note that you ONLY PRESS the EXP (or EE) button — you DON'T press X or 10 at all.

## 2) Reading Standard Form Numbers:

The big thing you have to remember when you write any standard form number from the calculator display is to put the "×10" in yourself. DON'T just write down what it says on the display.

### Example: *"Write down the number* | 7.986 $^{05}$ | *as a finished answer."*

As a finished answer this must be written as 7.986 × 10$^5$.

It is NOT 7.986$^5$ so DON'T write it down like that — YOU have to put the × 10$^n$ in yourself, even though it isn't shown in the display at all. *That's the bit people forget.*

## The Acid Test: LEARN the Three Rules and the Two Calculator Methods, then turn over and write them down.

Now cover up these 2 pages and answer these:
1) What are the Three Rules for standard form?
2) Express 958,000 in standard index form.     3) And the same for 0.00018
4) Express 4.56 × 10$^3$ as an ordinary number.
5) Work this out using your calculator: 3.2 × 10$^{12}$ ÷ 1.6 × 10$^{-9}$ , and write down the answer, first in standard form and then as an ordinary number.

# Ratios

The whole grisly subject of <u>RATIOS</u> gets a whole lot easier when you do this:

## Treat RATIOS like FRACTIONS

So for the <u>RATIO</u> 3:4, you'd treat it as the <u>FRACTION</u> 3/4, which is 0.75 as a <u>DECIMAL</u>.

### What the fraction form of the ratio actually means

Suppose in a class there's <u>girls and boys</u> in the ratio 3 : 4.
This means there's 3/4 as many girls as boys.
So if there were 20 boys, there would be 3/4 × 20 = 15 girls.
You've got to be careful — it <u>doesn't mean</u> 3/4 of the <u>people</u> in the class are girls.

# Reducing Ratios to their simplest form

You reduce ratios just like you'd reduce fractions to their simplest form.

For the ratio 15 : 18, both numbers have a <u>factor</u> of 3, so <u>divide them by 3</u> —
That gives 5 : 6. We can't reduce this any further, so the simplest form of 15 : 18 is <u>5 : 6</u>.

### Treat them just like fractions — use your calculator if you can

Now this is really sneaky. If you stick in a fraction using the $a^b_c$ button, your calculator automatically cancels it down when you press =.
So for the ratio 8 : 12, just press 8 $a^b_c$ 12 = , and you'll get the reduced fraction 2/3.
Now you just change it back to ratio form ie. <u>2 : 3</u>. Ace.

# The More Awkward Cases:

### 1) The $a^b_c$ button will only accept whole numbers

So <u>IF THE RATIO IS AWKWARD</u> (like "2.4 : 3.6" or "1¼ : 3½") then you must:
<u>MULTIPLY BOTH SIDES</u> by the <u>SAME NUMBER</u> until they are both <u>WHOLE NUMBERS</u>
and then you can use the $a^b_c$ button as before to simplify them down.
e.g. with "1¼ : 3½", × both sides by 4 gives "<u>5 : 14</u>" (Try $a^b_c$, but it won't cancel further)

### 2) If the ratio is MIXED UNITS

then you must <u>CONVERT BOTH SIDES</u> into the <u>SMALLER UNITS</u> using the
relevant <u>CONVERSION FACTOR</u> (see P.34), and then carry on as normal.
e.g. "24mm : 7.2cm" (× 7.2cm by 10) ⇒ 24mm : 72mm = <u>1 : 3</u> (using $a^b_c$)

### 3) To reduce a ratio to the form 1 : n        (n can be any number at all)

Simply <u>DIVIDE BOTH SIDES BY THE SMALLEST SIDE</u>.
e.g. take "3 : 56" — dividing both sides by 3 gives: <u>1 : 18.7</u> (56÷3) (i.e. 1 : n)
The 1 : n form is often the <u>most useful</u>, since it shows the ratio very clearly.

# Ratios

## Using the Formula Triangle in Ratio Questions

*"Mortar is made from sand and cement in the ratio 7:2.*
*If 9 buckets of sand are used, how much cement is needed?"*

This is a fairly common type of Exam question and it's pretty tricky for most people
— but once you start using the formula triangle method, it's all a bit of a breeze really.

This is the basic **FORMULA TRIANGLE** for **RATIOS**, but **NOTE:**

1) **THE RATIO MUST BE THE RIGHT WAY ROUND,**
   with the **FIRST NUMBER IN THE RATIO** relating to
   the item **ON TOP** in the triangle.

2) You'll always need to **CONVERT THE RATIO** into its
   **EQUIVALENT FRACTION** or Decimal to work out the answer.

The formula triangle for the mortar question is shown below and the trick is to replace
the **RATIO** 7:2 by its **EQUIVALENT FRACTION**:  7/2, or **3.5** as a decimal (7÷2)

So, *covering up cement in the triangle*, gives us "cement = sand / (7:2)"
i.e.  "9 / 3.5" = 9 ÷ 3.5 = **2.57** or about *2½ buckets of cement.*

## Proportional Division

In a *proportional division question* a *TOTAL AMOUNT* is to be *split in a certain ratio*.

For example:  *"£9100 is to be split in the ratio 2:4:7.  Find the 3 amounts".*

The key word here is **PARTS**. — concentrate on "parts" and it all becomes quite painless:

### Method:

1) **ADD UP THE PARTS:**
   The ratio 2:4:7 means there will be a total of 13 *parts*    i.e.  2+4+7 = **13 PARTS**

2) **FIND THE AMOUNT FOR ONE "PART"**
   Just *divide* the *total amount* by the number of *parts:*   £9100 ÷ 13 = **£700**    (= 1 PART)

3) **HENCE FIND THE THREE AMOUNTS:**
   2 parts = 2×700 = **£1400**,      4 parts = 4×700 = **£2800**,      7 parts = 4×700 = **£4900**

## The Acid Test:

LEARN the **6 RULES** for **SIMPLIFYING**, the
**FORMULA TRIANGLE** for Ratios (plus 2 points),
and the **3 Steps** for **PROPORTIONAL DIVISION**.

Now *turn over* and *write down what you've learned.*  Try again *until you can do it.*

1) Simplify:   a) **25:35**    b) **3.4 : 5.1**    c) **2¼ : 3¾**
2) Porridge and ice cream are mixed in the ratio 7:4 .  How much porridge should go with
   10 bowls of ice cream?         3) Divide £8400 in the ratio  **5:3:4**

# Rearranging Formulas

*Rearranging Formulas* means making one letter the subject, e.g. getting "y= " from something like $2x + z = 3(y + 2p)$. Generally speaking "solving equations" is easier, but don't forget:

1) EXACTLY THE SAME METHOD APPLIES TO BOTH FORMULAS AND EQUATIONS. (See P.21)
2) THE SAME SEQUENCE OF STEPS APPLIES EVERY TIME.

We'll illustrate this by making "y" the subject of this formula:   $M = \sqrt{2K - \dfrac{K^2}{2y + 1}}$

## The Six Steps Applied to Formulas

1) Get rid of any square root signs by <u>squaring both sides</u>:   $M^2 = 2K - \dfrac{K^2}{2y + 1}$

2) Get everything off the bottom by <u>cross-multiplying up to EVERY OTHER TERM</u>:

$$M^2 = 2K \ \overset{\displaystyle\leftarrow}{\underset{\displaystyle\leftarrow}{}} \ \frac{K^2}{2y + 1} \quad \Rightarrow \quad M^2(2y + 1) = 2K(2y + 1) - K^2$$

3) Multiply out any brackets:   $2yM^2 + M^2 = 4Ky + 2K - K^2$

4) Collect all <u>subject terms</u> on one side of the "="
   and all <u>non-subject terms</u> on the other side,
   <u>remembering to reverse the +/– sign of any term that crosses the "="</u>:

+4Ky moves across the "=" and becomes –4Ky
+M² moves across the "=" and becomes –M²

$$2yM^2 - 4Ky = -M^2 + 2K - K^2$$

5) <u>Combine together like terms</u> on each side of the equation, and reduce it to
   the form "<u>Ax = B</u>", where A and B are just bunches of letters which DON'T
   include the subject (y). Note that the LHS has to be <u>FACTORISED</u>:

$$(2M^2 - 4K)y = 2K - K^2 - M^2$$
$$(\text{"Ax = B" i.e. } A = (2M^2 - 4K),\ B = 2K - K^2 - M^2,\ y \text{ is the subject })$$

6) Finally <u>slide the A underneath the B</u> to give "$X = \frac{B}{A}$",
   (cancel if possible) and that's your answer:   So   $y = \dfrac{2K - K^2 - M^2}{(2M^2 - 4K)}$

## And One Extra Thing...

If you find yourself having to solve for a
*squared coefficient* then treat it just like
normal (i.e. put $x^2$ = a random variable,
say 'P') then at the end, just take the
*square root* of the other side — simple!
Try and follow this example through:

Solve for x:
$$y = 3K + \frac{2x^2 - 3L}{2}$$

$$\Rightarrow y = 3K + \frac{2P - 3L}{2}$$

> I've missed out a load of
> steps here, but you should be
> able to work out what I did by
> looking through the stuff
> above.

$$\Rightarrow P = \frac{2(y - 3K) + 3L}{2} = x^2 \Rightarrow x = \sqrt{\frac{2(y - 3K) + 3L}{2}}$$

## The Acid Test:
LEARN the <u>6 STEPS</u> for <u>rearranging formulas</u>.
Turn over and write them down.

1) Rearrange "$F = \frac{9}{5}C + 32$" from "F= " to "C= " and then back the other way.
2) Make p the subject of these:   a) $\dfrac{p}{p + y} = 4$   b) $y = x^2p^2 - 3p^2$

# Inequalities

This is basically quite difficult, but it's still worth learning the easy bits in case they ask a very easy question on it, as well they might. Here are the easy bits:

## The 4 Inequality Symbols:

> means "Greater than"    ≥ means "Greater than or equal to"
< means "Less than"    ≤ means "Less than or equal to"

REMEMBER, the one at the BIG end is BIGGEST

so "X > 4" and "4 < X" BOTH say: "X is greater than 4"

## Algebra with Inequalities — this is generally a bit tricky

The thing to remember here is that inequalities are just like regular equations:

$$5X < X + 2$$
$$5X = X + 2$$

in the sense that all the normal rules of algebra (see P.17-P.19) apply...

...BUT WITH ONE BIG EXCEPTION:

Whenever you MULTIPLY OR DIVIDE BY A NEGATIVE NUMBER, you must FLIP THE INEQUALITY SIGN.

### Example: "Solve 5X < 6X + 2"

ANS:    First move the 6X over the "=" :    $5X - 6X < 2$

combining the X-terms gives:    $-X < 2$

To get rid of the "−" in front of X you need to divide both sides by −1 — but remember that means the "<" has to be flipped as well, which gives:

$X > -2$    i.e. "X is greater than −2" is the answer

(The < has flipped around into a >, because we divided by a −ve number)

This answer, X > −2, can be displayed as a shaded region on a number line like this:

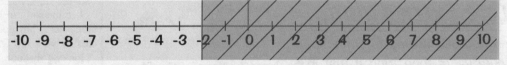

The main thing you should realise, is that MOST OF THE TIME you just treat the "<" or ">" as though it was an "=" and do all the usual algebra that you would for a regular equation. The "Big Exception" doesn't actually come up very often at all.

## The Acid Test:

LEARN: The 4 Inequality Symbols, the similarity with EQUATIONS and the One Big Exception.

Now turn over and write down what you've learned.

1) Solve this inequality:    $4X + 3 \leq 6X + 7$ .

2) Find all the integer values of X which satisfy both   $2X + 9 \geq 1$   and   $4X < 6 + X$

# Trial and Improvement

In principle, this is an easy way to find approximate answers to quite complicated equations, especially "cubics" (ones with $x^3$ in). BUT... you have to make an effort to <u>LEARN THE FINER DETAILS</u> of this method, otherwise you'll never get the hang of it.

## Method

1) <u>SUBSTITUTE TWO INITIAL VALUES</u> into the equation that give <u>OPPOSITE CASES</u>. These are usually suggested in the question. If not, you'll have to think of your own. Opposite cases means <u>one answer too big, one too small</u>, or <u>one +ve, one –ve</u>, for example. If they don't give opposite cases <u>try again</u>.

2) Now **CHOOSE YOUR NEXT VALUE <u>IN BETWEEN</u> THE PREVIOUS TWO,** and <u>SUBSTITUTE it into the equation</u>.
   <u>Continue this process</u>, always choosing a new value <u>between the two closest opposite cases</u> (and preferably nearer to the one which is closest to the answer you want).

3) <u>AFTER ONLY 3 OR 4 STEPS</u> you should have <u>2 numbers</u> which are to the <u>right degree of accuracy but DIFFER BY 1 IN THE LAST DIGIT</u>.
   For example if you had to get your answer to 2 d.p. then you'd eventually end up with say 5.43 and 5.44, with these giving **OPPOSITE** results of course.

4) <u>At this point</u> you ALWAYS take the <u>Exact Middle Value</u> to decide which is the answer you want. e.g. for 5.43 and 5.44, you'd try 5.435 to see if the real answer was <u>between 5.43 and 5.435</u> or between <u>5.435 and 5.44</u> (see below).

## Example

*The equation $X^3 + X = 40$ has a solution between 3 and 3.5. Find this solution to 1 d.p.*

| Try X = 3 | $3^3 + 3 = 30$ | (Too small) | ← (2 opposite cases) |
| Try X = 3.5 | $3.5^3 + 3.5 = 46.375$ | (Too big) | |

40 is what we want and it's closer to 46.375 than it is to 30 so we'll choose our next value for X closer to 3.5 than 3

| Try X = 3.3 | $3.3^3 + 3.3 = 39.237$ | (Too small) |

*Good*, this is very close, but we need to see if 3.4 is still too big or too small:

| Try X = 3.4 | $3.4^3 + 3.4 = 42.704$ | (Too big) |

*Good*, now we know that <u>the answer must be between 3.3 and 3.4</u>. To find out which one it's nearest to, we have to try the <u>EXACT MIDDLE VALUE</u>: 3.35

| Try X = 3.35 | $3.35^3 + 3.35 = 40.945$ (Too big) |

This tells us with certainty that the solution must be between 3.3 (too small) and 3.35 (too big), and so to 1 d.p. <u>it must round down to 3.3.</u>ANSWER = 3.3

## The Acid Test:
"LEARN and TURN" — if you don't actually <u>commit it to memory</u>, then you've wasted your time even reading it.

To succeed with this method you must <u>LEARN the 4 steps above</u>. Do it now, and practise until you can <u>write them down without having to look back at them</u>. It's not as difficult as you think.

1) The equation $X^3 - 2X = 1$ has a solution between 1 and 2. Find it to 1 d.p.

# Finding the Gradient of a Line

Working out the gradient of a straight line is a slightly involved business, and there are quite a few things that can go wrong.

Once again though, if you _learn and follow the steps below_ and treat it as a <u>STRICT METHOD</u>, you'll have a lot more success than if you try and fudge your way through it, like you usually do.

## Strict Method For Finding Gradient

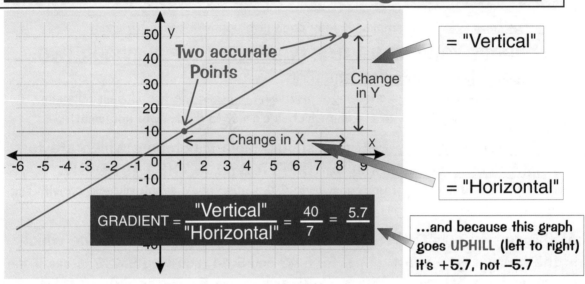

$$\text{GRADIENT} = \frac{\text{"Vertical"}}{\text{"Horizontal"}} = \frac{40}{7} = 5.7$$

...and because this graph goes UPHILL (left to right) it's +5.7, not –5.7

### 1) Find <u>TWO ACCURATE POINTS</u>, reasonably far apart

Both in the _upper right quadrant_ if possible, (to keep all the numbers positive and so reduce the chance of errors).

### 2) <u>_COMPLETE THE TRIANGLE_</u> as shown

### 3) Find the <u>CHANGE IN Y</u> and the <u>CHANGE IN X</u>

Make sure you do this _using the SCALES on the Y- and X- axes_, <u>not by counting cm</u>! (So in the example shown, the Change in Y is NOT 4cm, but _40 units_ off the Y-axis.)

### 4) <u>LEARN</u> this formula, and use it:

$$\text{GRADIENT} = \frac{\text{VERTICAL}}{\text{HORIZONTAL}}$$

Make sure you get it the right way up too!
Remember it's
<u>VER</u>y <u>HO</u>t — <u>VER</u>tical over <u>HO</u>rizontal

### 5) Finally, is the gradient <u>_POSITIVE_</u> or <u>_NEGATIVE_</u>?

If it slopes <u>UPHILL</u> left → right ( ⟋ ) <u>then it's +ve</u>
If it slopes <u>DOWNHILL</u> left → right ( ⟍ ) <u>then it's –ve</u> (so put a minus(–) in front of it)

## The Acid Test:
<u>LEARN</u> the <u>FIVE STEPS</u> for finding a gradient then <u>turn over</u> and <u>WRITE THEM DOWN</u> from memory.

1) Plot these 3 points on a graph: (0,3) (2,0) (5,-4.5) and then join them up with a straight line. Now carefully apply the <u>FIVE STEPS</u> to find the gradient of the line.

# Plotting Straight Line Graphs

A lot of people wouldn't know a straight line equation if it ran up and bit them, but they're pretty easy to spot really — they just have _two letters_ and _a few numbers_, but with _nothing fancy_ like squared or cubed.   (Now that you're inflamed with burning curiosity, look at P.77 to see some examples)

Anyway, in the Exam you'll be expected to draw the graph of a straight line equation.
"y = mx + c" is the hard way of doing it (see P.52).  Here's the EASY WAY of doing it:

## The "Table of 3 Values" method

You can **EASILY** draw the graph of **ANY EQUATION** using this **EASY** method.

### Method:

1) Choose **3 VALUES OF X** and draw up a table,

2) **WORK OUT THE VALUE OF Y** for each value of X.

3) **PLOT THE COORDINATES**, and **DRAW THE LINE**.

_If it's a straight line equation, the 3 points will be in a dead straight line with each other, which is the usual check you do when you've drawn it._
_If they aren't, then it could be a curve and you'll need to do more values in your table to find out what's going on._

### Example:  "Draw the graph of Y = 2X – 3".

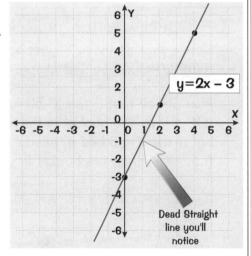

y=2x – 3

Dead Straight line you'll notice

1) **DRAW UP A TABLE** with some _suitable values_ of **X**.
   Choosing  **X = 0, 2, 4** is usually cool enough.
   i.e.

| X | 0 | 2 | 4 |
|---|---|---|---|
| Y |   |   |   |

2) **FIND THE Y-VALUES** by putting each x-value into the equation:

   e.g. When  $\underline{X = 4}$,
   y = 2X – 3
   = 2×4 – 3
   = 8 – 3   = $\underline{5}$

| X | 0 | 2 | 4 |
|---|---|---|---|
| Y | -3 | 1 | 5 |

3) **PLOT THE POINTS** and **DRAW THE LINE** right across the graph (as shown).

   (The points should always lie in a **DEAD STRAIGHT LINE**.  If they don't, do more values in the table to find out what on earth's happening.)

## The Acid Test:   LEARN the details of this _easy method_ then _turn over and write them all down._

1) Draw the graphs of     a)  y = 4 + x      b)  y = 3x + 2      c) y = 6 – 2x

# Straight Lines and Quadratics

## Using $y = mx + c$

$y = mx + c$ is the general equation for a straight line graph, and you need to remember:

> "m" is equal to the __GRADIENT__ of the graph
>
> "c" is the value __WHERE IT CROSSES THE Y-AXIS__ and is called the __INTERCEPT__.

## 1) Drawing a Straight Line using "y = mx + c"

The main thing is being able to identify "m" and "c" and knowing what to do with them:
BUT WATCH OUT — people often mix up "m" and "c", especially with say, "y = 5 + 2x"
__REMEMBER__: "m" is the number __IN FRONT OF X__ and "c" is the number __ON ITS OWN__.

### Method

1) Get the equation into the form "$y = mx + c$".

2) __IDENTIFY__ "m" and "c" __CAREFULLY__.

3) __PUT A DOT ON THE Y-AXIS__ at the value of c.

4) Then go __ALONG ONE UNIT__ and _up or down by the value of m_ and make another dot.

5) __Repeat__ the same "step" in _both directions_ as shown:

6) Finally __CHECK__ that the gradient __LOOKS RIGHT__.

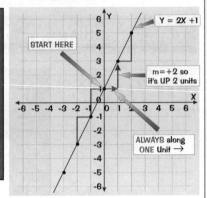

START HERE

Y = 2X +1

m=+2 so it's UP 2 units

ALWAYS along ONE Unit →

_The graph shows the process for the equation "y = 2x + 1":_

1) "c" = 1, so put a first dot at y = 1 on the y-axis.
2) Go along 1 unit → and then up by 2 because "m" = +2.
3) Repeat the same step, 1→ 2↑ in _both_ directions. (i.e. 1 ← 2 ↓ the other way)
4) CHECK: _a gradient of +2 should be quite steep and uphill left to right_ — which it is.

## 2) $X^2$ Bucket Shapes:

Y = anything with $X^2$ in it, but not $X^3$

Notice that all these $X^2$ graphs have the _same_ SYMMETRICAL bucket shape.

Also notice that if the $X^2$ bit is positive (i.e. $+X^2$ ) then the bucket is the normal way up, but if the $X^2$ bit has a "minus" in front of it (i.e. $-X^2$ ) then the bucket is _upside down_.

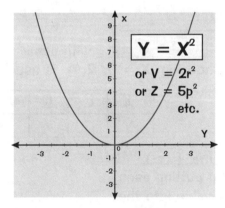

$Y = X^2$

or $V = 2r^2$
or $Z = 5p^2$
etc.

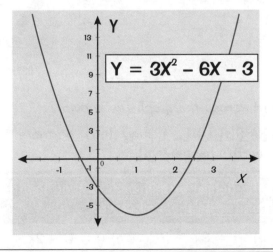

$Y = 3X^2 - 6X - 3$

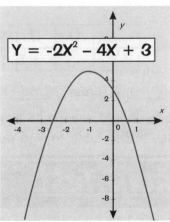

$Y = -2X^2 - 4X + 3$

# Typical Graph Questions

There's a lot of fiddly details involved in graph questions: getting the right values in the table; plotting the right points; and getting the final answers from your graph.
If you want to get all these easy marks, then you've got to learn all these little tricks:

## Filling in The Table of Values

A typical question:   *"Complete the table of values for the equation $y = x^2 - 4x + 3$"*

| x | -2 | -1 | 0 | 1 | 2 | 3 | 4 | 5 | 6 |
|---|----|----|---|---|---|---|---|---|---|
| y |    |    |   | 0 |   |   | 3 |   | 15 |

<u>WHAT YOU DON'T DO</u> is try to punch it all into the calculator in one go. Not good. The rest of the question hinges on this table of values and one silly mistake here could cost you a lot of marks. This might look like a long-winded method but it takes far less time than you think and is the only <u>REALLY SAFE</u> method.

### 1) For EVERY value in the table you should WRITE THIS OUT:

<u>For x=4:</u>   $y = x^2 - 4x + 3$      <u>For x=-1:</u>   $y = x^2 - 4x + 3$
                $= 4^2 - 4 \times 4 + 3$                      $= (-1 \times -1) - (4 \times -1) + 3$
                $= 16 - 16 + 3$                      $= 1 - -4 + 3 = 1 + 4 + 3$
                $= \underline{3}$                      $= \underline{8}$

### 2) Make sure you can reproduce the y-values they've already given you...

— *BEFORE you fill in the spaces in the table.* This is really important to make sure you're doing it right, before you start cheerfully working out a pile of wrong values!

I wouldn't tell you all this without good reason, so ignore it at your peril.

## Plotting the Points and Drawing the Curve

Here again there are easy marks to be won and lost — this all matters:

1) <u>GET THE AXES THE RIGHT WAY ROUND</u>: The values from the <u>FIRST row or column</u> are ALWAYS plotted *on the X-axis*.

2) <u>PLOT THE POINTS CAREFULLY</u>, and don't mix up the x and y values.

3) The points will **ALWAYS** form a <u>DEAD STRAIGHT LINE</u> or a <u>COMPLETELY SMOOTH CURVE</u>.

   If they don't, they're *wrong*.

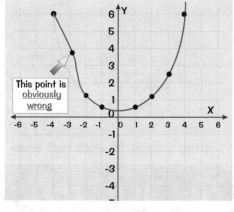

This point is obviously wrong

4) A graph from an <u>ALGEBRA EQUATION</u> must always be drawn as a <u>SMOOTH CURVE</u> (or a dead straight line). You only use lots of short straight line sections to join points in *"Data Handling"* when it's called a "frequency polygon". (See P.64)

<u>NEVER EVER</u> *let one point drag your line off* in some ridiculous direction — if one point seems out of place, *check the value in the table* and then check the position where you've plotted it. When a graph is generated from an equation, *you never get spikes or lumps* — only MISTAKES.

# Typical Graph Questions

## Getting Answers from Your Graph

1) <u>FOR A SINGLE CURVE OR LINE</u>, you <u>ALWAYS</u> get the answer by *drawing a straight line to the graph from one axis, and then down or across to the other axis*, as shown here:

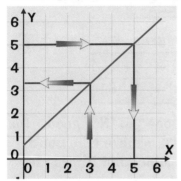

You should be *fully expecting* this to happen so that even if you don't understand the question, you can still have a pretty good stab at it:

If the question said *"Find the value of y when x is equal to 3"*, <u>ALL YOU DO IS THIS</u>: *start at 3 on the x-axis, go straight up to the graph, then straight over to the y-axis and read off the value, which in this case is <u>y = 3.2</u>* (as shown opposite).

2) <u>IF TWO LINES CROSS.....</u>

you can bet your very last fruitcake the answer to one of the questions will simply be:
<u>THE VALUES OF X AND Y WHERE THEY CROSS</u>.
(You'll do all about this sort of thing in Stage 3 — see Simultaneous Eqns. P.74 and P.75).

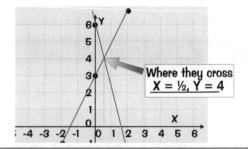

Where they cross
X = ½, Y = 4

## What The Gradient of a Graph MEANS

No matter what the graph, <u>THE MEANING OF THE GRADIENT</u> is always simply:

### (Y-axis UNITS)   PER   (X-axis UNITS)

*EXAMPLES:*

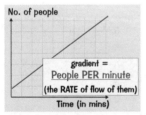

No. of people

gradient =
People PER minute
(the RATE of flow of them)
Time (in mins)

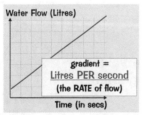

Water Flow (Litres)

gradient =
Litres PER second
(the RATE of flow)
Time (in secs)

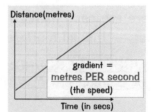

Distance(metres)

gradient =
metres PER second
(the speed)
Time (in secs)

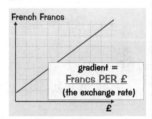

French Francs

gradient =
Francs PER £
(the exchange rate)
£

Some gradients have special names like *Exchange Rate* or *Speed*, but once you've written down *"something PER something"* using the Y-axis and X-axis <u>UNITS</u>, it's then pretty easy to work out what the gradient represents.

## The Acid Test:

LEARN the <u>2 Rules for doing tables of values</u>, the <u>4 points for drawing graphs</u>, the <u>2 simple Rules for getting answers</u>, and <u>the meaning of gradient</u>.

Now turn over and *write it all down from memory*. Then *try again until you can do it*.

1) *Complete the table of values* at the top of the previous page (using the proper methods!), and then *draw the graph* taking note of the Four Points.
2) From your graph <u>find the value of y when x is 4.2</u>, and <u>the values of x when y=12</u>.
3) If I drew a graph of "miles covered" up the y-axis and "gallons used" along the x-axis, and worked out the gradient, what would the value of it tell me?

# Pythagoras' Theorem

1) <u>PYTHAGORAS' THEOREM</u> goes hand in hand with SIN, COS and TAN (see next page) because they're both involved with <u>RIGHT-ANGLED TRIANGLES</u>.

2) The big difference is that <u>PYTHAGORAS DOES NOT INVOLVE ANY ANGLES</u> — it just uses *two sides* to find the *third side*. (SIN, COS and TAN always involve <u>ANGLES</u>.)

## *Method*   The basic formula for Pythagoras' theorem is:   $a^2 + b^2 = h^2$

Remember that Pythagoras can only be used on <u>RIGHT-ANGLED TRIANGLES</u>.

The trouble is, the formula can be quite difficult to use. *Instead*, it's a lot better to *just remember* these *THREE SIMPLE STEPS*, which work every time:

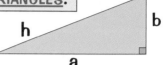

### *1) Square Them*   SQUARE THE TWO NUMBERS that you are given,

(use the $x^2$ button if you've got your calculator — if you haven't, make sure you know the squares on P.6)

### *2) Add or Subtract*   To find the *longest side*, ADD the two squared numbers.

To find *a shorter side*, SUBTRACT the smaller one from the larger.

### *3) Square Root*   Once you've got your answer, take the SQUARE ROOT.

(By pressing $\sqrt{}$, then checking that your answer is <u>SENSIBLE</u>, or by *remembering everything on P.6*.)

## *Example 1:*   *"Find the missing side in the triangle shown."*

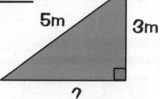

**ANSWER:** ❶   Square them:  $5^2 = 25$,  $3^2 = 9$

❷   You want to find a <u>shorter side</u>,

so <u>SUBTRACT</u>:   $25 - 9 = 16$

❸   Square root:  $\sqrt{16} = 4$   So the <u>missing side = 4m</u>

(You should always ask yourself:   "Is it a *sensible answer*?" — in this case you can say "<u>YES</u>, because it's shorter than 5m, as it should be since 5m is the longest side, but not too much shorter")

## *Example 2:*   *"Find the length of the line segment shown."* For coordinates, see P.24

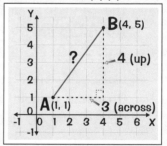

**ANSWER:** ❶   Work out <u>how far across and up</u> it is from <u>A to B</u>

❷   Treat this exactly like a <u>normal triangle</u>...

❸   Square them:  $3^2 = 9$,  $4^2 = 16$

❹   You want to find the <u>longer side</u> (the hypotenuse), so <u>ADD</u>:   $9 + 16 = 25$

❺   Square root:  $\sqrt{25} = 5$

So the <u>length of the line segment = 5 units</u>

## The Acid Test:

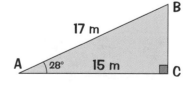

1) Apply the above method to find the missing side BC:

2) Another triangle has sides of 5 m, 12 m and 13 m. Is it a right-angled triangle? How do you know?

# Trigonometry — SIN, COS, TAN

Using formula triangles to do Trigonometry makes the whole thing _a whole lot easier_, but ALWAYS follow all these steps in this order.  If you miss any out _you're asking for trouble_.

## Method
Using SIN, COS and TAN to solve right-angled triangles

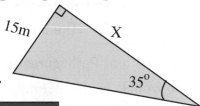

**1)**  Label the three sides O, A and H

(Opposite, Adjacent and Hypotenuse).

**2)**  Write down **FROM MEMORY**  "SOH CAH TOA"

(Sounds like a Chinese word, "Sockatoa!")

**3)**  Decide **WHICH TWO SIDES are involved**  O,H  A,H  or  O,A

and select S**OH**, C**AH** or T**OA** accordingly

**4)**  Turn the one you choose into a **FORMULA TRIANGLE**, thus:

**5)**  Cover up the thing you want to find

with your finger, and write down whatever is left showing.

**6)**  Translate into numbers and work it out

**7)**  Finally, check that your answer is _sensible_.

## Seven Nitty Gritty Details

☺  The HYPOTENUSE is the LONGEST SIDE.
The OPPOSITE is the side OPPOSITE the angle being used (θ).
The ADJACENT is the side NEXT TO the angle being used (θ).

☺  θ IS A GREEK LETTER called "theta", _and is used to represent ANGLES_

☺  In the formula triangles, $S^\theta$ represents **SIN** θ, $C^\theta$ is **COS** θ, and $T^\theta$ is **TAN** θ.

☺  On some calculators, you have to enter trig functions BACKWARDS.
So for SIN 45 you might have to press  45  SIN  (but most calculators do it the right way now).

☺  Remember, TO FIND THE ANGLE — USE INVERSE  (see opposite page →).

☺  ALWAYS USE A DIAGRAM — _draw your own if necessary_.

☺  You can only use SIN, COS and TAN on RIGHT-ANGLED TRIANGLES — you may have to _add lines to the diagram to create one_ — especially on ISOSCELES triangles.

## The Acid Test:
LEARN the 7 Steps of the Method and....
...the 7 Nitty Gritty Details.

Then turn over and write them all down from memory.

# Trigonometry — SIN, COS, TAN

---

### Example 1)    "_Find x in the triangle shown_."

1) Label O,A,H
2) Write down "SOH CAH TOA"
3) Two sides _involved_: O,H

4) So use

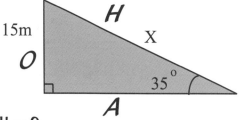

5) We want to find H so cover it up to leave:    $H = \dfrac{O}{S^\theta}$
6) Substitute in values:

$$X = \dfrac{15}{SIN\ 35}$$

Press   [15] [÷] [SIN] [35] [=]    `26.151702`    So answer = <u>26.2m</u>

7) Check it's sensible: yes it's about twice as big as 15, as the diagram suggests.

---

### Example 2)    "_Find the angle θ in this triangle_."

_Note the usual way of dealing with an ISOSCELES TRIANGLE: split it down the middle to get a RIGHT ANGLE:_

1) Label O, A, H
2) Write down "SOH CAH TOA'"
3) Two sides _involved_: A,H

4) So use

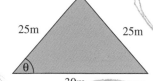
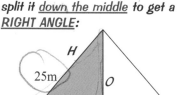

5) We want to find θ so cover up Cθ to leave:    $C\theta = \dfrac{A}{H}$

6) Substitute in values:    $COS\ \theta = \dfrac{15}{25} = 0.6$

<u>NOW USE INVERSE</u> :     θ = INV COS (0.6)

Press   [INV] [COS] [0.6] [=]    `53.130102`    So ans. = <u>53.1°</u>

7) Finally, is it sensible? — Yes, the angle looks like about 50°.

---

## Angles of _Elevation_ **and** _Depression_

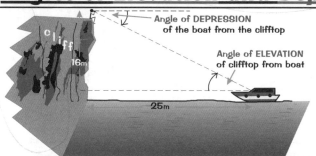

Angle of DEPRESSION of the boat from the clifftop

Angle of ELEVATION of clifftop from boat

1) The _Angle of Depression_ is the angle _downwards_ from the horizontal.

2) The _Angle of Elevation_ is the angle _upwards_ from the horizontal.

3) The _Angle of Elevation_ and _Angle of Depression_ are <u>ALWAYS EQUAL</u>.

---

## The Acid Test:    <u>Practise these questions</u> until you can apply the method <u>fluently</u> and without having to refer to it <u>at all</u>.

1) Find **X**

2) Find θ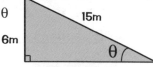

3) Calculate the angles of elevation and depression in the boat drawing above.

# Circle Geometry

# Three Simple Rules — that's all:

You'll have to learn these if you want to be able to do circle problems.

## 1) TANGENT and RADIUS MEET AT 90°

A TANGENT is a line that just touches the edge of a curve. <u>If a tangent and radius meet</u> at the same point, then the angle they make is *EXACTLY 90°*.

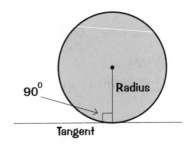

90°      Radius

Tangent

## 2) EQUALITY OF TANGENTS FROM A POINT

The two tangents drawn from an outside point are <u>always equal in length</u>, so creating an "isosceles" situation, with <u>two congruent right-angled triangles</u>.

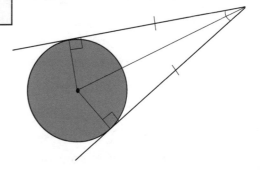

## 3) INSCRIBED REGULAR POLYGONS

1) You can draw regular polygons by dividing a circle into <u>equal sections</u>.

2) All you have to do is <u>join up</u> where the sections meet the circle.

### Examples

To make a <u>3-sided</u> regular polygon (equilateral triangle):
360° ÷ 3 = 120°
so we need <u>3 sections of 120°</u>...

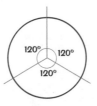

...and then just join up the points.

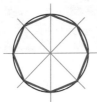

<u>8-sided</u> regular polygon (octogon):
360° ÷ 8 = 45°
so <u>8 sections of 45°</u>

<u>4-sided</u> regular polygon (square):
360° ÷ 4 = 90°
so <u>4 sections of 90°</u>

# Enlargements — The 4 Key Features

**1)** If the <u>Scale Factor is BIGGER THAN 1</u> then <u>the shape gets BIGGER</u>.

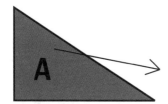

A to B is an Enlargement, Scale Factor 1½

**2)** If the <u>Scale Factor is SMALLER than 1</u> (i.e. a fraction like ½), then the <u>shape gets SMALLER</u>.

A to B is an Enlargement of Scale Factor ½

(Really this is a *reduction*, but you still call it an <u>Enlargement, Scale Factor ½</u>)

**3)** Enlargement Scale Factor 3

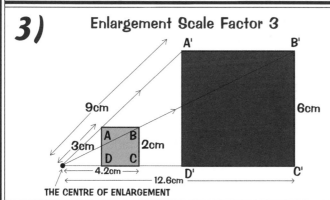

THE CENTRE OF ENLARGEMENT

The <u>Scale Factor</u> also tells you the <u>RELATIVE DISTANCE</u> of old points and new points <u>from the Centre of Enlargement</u>.

This is <u>VERY USEFUL FOR DRAWING AN ENLARGEMENT</u>, because you can use it to <u>trace out the positions of the new points</u> from the centre of enlargement, as shown in the diagram.

**4)** The lengths of the big and small shapes <u>are related to the Scale Factor</u> by this <u>VERY important Formula Triangle WHICH YOU MUST LEARN</u>:

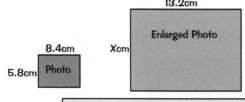

Obviously, if the length of a single side is multiplied by the scale factor, then the perimeter will also change by the same amount — e.g. a square of side-length 1 enlarged by scale factor 2 will have sides of length 2 and a perimeter changed from 4 to 8 (4 × 2).

- - - - - - - - - - - - - - - - - - - - - - - - - - - - - - - - - - - - - - - - - - -

This now lets you to tackle <u>the classic "Enlarged photo"</u> <u>Exam question</u> with breathtaking triviality:

To find the width of the enlarged photo we <u>use the formula triangle TWICE</u> (firstly to find the Scale Factor, and then to find the <u>missing side</u>):

1) <u>Scale Factor</u> = New length ÷ Old length = 13.2 ÷ 8.4 = <u>1.57</u>
2) <u>New width</u>  =  Scale Factor × Old width = 1.57 × 5.8 = <u>9.1 cm</u>

***BUT WITHOUT THE FORMULA TRIANGLE YOU'RE SCUPPERED!***

## The Acid Test:

<u>LEARN</u> the <u>FOUR KEY FEATURES</u> of enlargements, especially the <u>FORMULA TRIANGLE</u>.

Then, <u>when you think you know it</u>, cover the page and <u>write it all down again</u>, from memory, including the sketches and examples, <u>especially the photo enlargement</u> one. Keep trying till you can.

# Density and Speed

You might think this is Physics, but density is specifically mentioned in the Maths syllabus, and it's very likely to come up in your Exam. The standard formula for density is:

## Density = Mass ÷ Volume

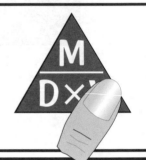

so we can put it in a FORMULA TRIANGLE like this:

*One way or another you MUST remember this formula for density, because they won't give it to you and without it you'll be pretty stuck. The best method by far is to remember the order of the letters in the FORMULA TRIANGLE as D^M V or DiMoV (The Russian Agent!).*

**EXAMPLE:** *"Find the volume of an object which has a mass of 40 g and a density of 6.4 g/cm³"*

ANSWER: To find volume, <u>cover up V</u> in the formula triangle. This leaves M/D showing, so V = M ÷ D
= 40÷6.4
= <u>6.25 cm³</u>

# Speed = Distance ÷ Time

This is very common. In fact it probably comes up every single year — *and they never give you the formula!* Either *learn it beforehand* or wave goodbye to *lots of easy marks.* Life isn't all bad though — there's an easy FORMULA TRIANGLE:

Of course you still have to <u>remember the order of the letters</u> in the triangle (S^D T) — but this time we have the word <u>SoDiT</u> to help you.

So if it's a question on speed, distance and time just say: **SOD IT**.

**EXAMPLE:** *"A car travels 90 miles at 36 miles per hour. How long does it take?"*

ANSWER: <u>We want to find the TIME</u>, so <u>cover up T</u> in the triangle which leaves D/S,

so   T = D/S   = Distance ÷ speed   = 90÷36 = <u>2.5 hours</u>

**LEARN THE <u>FORMULA TRIANGLE</u>, AND YOU'LL FIND QUESTIONS ON *SPEED, DISTANCE* AND *TIME* <u>VERY EASY</u>.**

# The Acid Test:
LEARN the formulas for **DENSITY** and **SPEED** — and also the two <u>Formula triangles</u>.

1) What's the formula triangle for Density?
2) A metal object has a volume of 45 cm³ and a mass of 743 g. What is its density?
3) Another piece of the same metal has a volume of 36.5 cm³. What is its mass?
4) What's the formula for speed, distance and time?
5) Find the time taken for a person walking at 3.2 km/h to cover 24 km.
   Also, find how far she'll walk in 3 hrs 30 mins.

# *Areas*

They don't promise to give you these formulas in the Exam, so if you don't learn them before you get there, you'll be SCUPPERED — simple as that.

## YOU MUST LEARN THESE FORMULAS:

## 1) *RECTANGLE*

Area of rectangle = Length × Width

Width

Length

$$A = L \times W$$

## 2) *TRIANGLE*

Area of triangle = ½ × Base x Vertical Height

$$A = \tfrac{1}{2} \times B \times H_v$$

Height

Base

*Right-angled triangles* are easy — just use the two short sides as shown above

Height

Base

For other triangles, the *height* must always be the *vertical height*, never the sloping height.

## 3) *CIRCLE*

### *DON'T MUDDLE UP THESE TWO CIRCLE FORMULAS!*

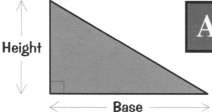

Radius

Diameter

CIRCUMFERENCE = distance round the outside of the circle

1) AREA of circle = π × (radius)²

$$A = \pi \times r^2$$

E.g. if the radius is 4cm
A = 3.14 x (4x4)
= 50cm²

2) CIRCUMFERENCE = π x Diameter

$$C = \pi \times D$$

E.g. if the radius is 4cm
Then diameter = 8cm,
C = 3.14 x 8
= 25.12cm

## *The Acid Test:*

### LEARN THE WHOLE OF THIS PAGE

Then turn over and write down as much as you can from memory. Then try again.

# _Volume or Capacity_

## VOLUMES — YOU MUST LEARN THESE TOO!

### 1) CUBOID (RECTANGULAR BLOCK)
(This is also known as a '_rectangular prism_' — see below to understand why)

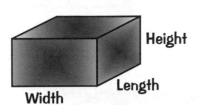

**Height**

**Length**

**Width**

Volume of Cuboid = length × width × height

$$V = l \times w \times h$$

(The other word for volume is _CAPACITY_)

### 2) PRISM

**A PRISM** is a solid (3-D) object which has a **CONSTANT AREA OF CROSS-SECTION** — i.e. it's the same shape all the way through.

Now, for some reason, not a lot of people know what a prism is, but they come up all the time in Exams, so make sure YOU know.

### Circular Prism
(or Cylinder)

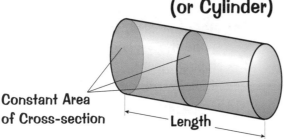

Constant Area of Cross-section

Length

### Hexagonal Prism
(a flat one, certainly, but still a prism)

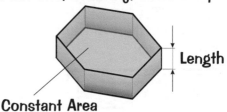

Length

Constant Area of Cross-section

### Triangular Prism

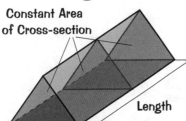

Constant Area of Cross-section

Length

Volume of prism = Cross-sectional Area × length

$$V = A \times l$$

As you can see, the formula for the volume of a prism is _very simple_. The _difficult_ part, usually, is _finding the area of the cross-section_.

## _The Acid Test:_
LEARN this page. Then turn over and try to write it all down. Keep trying until you can do it.

Practise these two questions until you can do them all the way through without any hesitation. Name the shapes and find their volumes:

a)

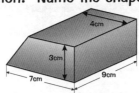

4cm

3cm

7cm

9cm

b)

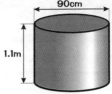

90cm

1.1m

# Pie Charts

They can make Pie Charts into quite tricky Exam questions.
So learn the Golden Rule for Pie Charts:

## The TOTAL of Everything = 360°

Remember that 360° is the trick for dealing with most Pie Charts

## 1) Relating Angles to Fractions

These five simplest ones you should just know straight off:

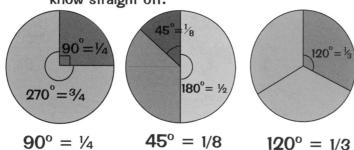

$$90° = ¼$$
$$270° = ¾$$
$$45° = 1/8$$
$$180° = ½$$
$$120° = 1/3$$

For any angle the formula is:

### Fraction = Angle / 360°

And then *cancel it down* with your calculator (see P.11)

If you have to measure an angle, you should expect it to be a nice round number like 90° or 180° or 120°, so don't go writing 89° or 181° or anything silly like that.

## 2) Relating angles to Numbers of other things

| Creature | Stick insects | Hamster | Guinea Pigs | Rabbits | Ducks | Total |
|----------|---------------|---------|-------------|---------|-------|-------|
| Number | 12 | 20 | 17 | 15 | 26 | 90 |

×4                    ×4

| Angle | | 80° | | | | 360° |
|-------|--|-----|--|--|--|------|

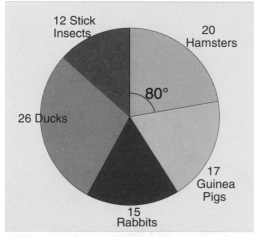

12 Stick Insects
20 Hamsters
80°
26 Ducks
17 Guinea Pigs
15 Rabbits

1) Add up all the numbers in each sector to get the TOTAL (← 90 for this one )

2) Then find the MULTIPLIER (or divider) that you need to *turn your total into 360°*:
For 90 → 360 as above, the MULTIPLIER is 4

3) Now MULTIPLY EVERY NUMBER BY 4 to get the angle for each sector.
E.g. the angle for hamsters will be
$$20 × 4 = \underline{80°}$$

## The Acid Test:

Display this data in a Pie Chart:

| Football Team | Wigan A. | Luton | Man.Utd. | Others |
|---------------|----------|-------|----------|--------|
| No. of Fans | 53 | 15 | 30 | 22 |

# Graphs and Charts

Make sure you know all these easy details:

## 1) Line Graphs or "Frequency Polygons"

A <u>line graph</u> or "<u>frequency polygon</u>" is just a set of points joined up with straight lines.

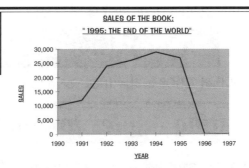

SALES OF THE BOOK:
"1995: THE END OF THE WORLD"

## 2) Scatter Graphs

1) <u>A SCATTER GRAPH</u> is just a load of points on a graph that <u>end up in a bit of a mess</u> rather than in a nice line or curve.

2) There's a fancy word to say <u>how much of a mess</u> they're in — it's <u>CORRELATION</u>.

3) <u>Good Correlation</u> (or <u>Strong</u> Correlation) means the points <u>form quite a nice line</u>, and it means <u>the two things are closely related to each other</u>.

4) The <u>LINE OF BEST FIT</u> goes roughly through the <u>middle</u> of the scatter of points.

5) If the line slopes <u>up</u>, it's <u>positive correlation</u>, if it slopes <u>down</u> it's <u>negative correlation</u>. <u>No correlation</u> means that there's no <u>LINEAR</u> relationship.

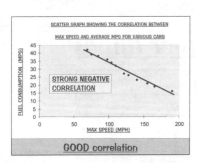

GOOD correlation

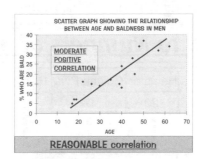

REASONABLE correlation

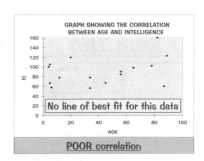

POOR correlation

## 3) Stem and Leaf Diagrams

<u>Stem and leaf</u> diagrams are a bit like bar charts, but more confusing. They're supposed to be easy to read, but they're not. So <u>LEARN</u> this example.

**EXAMPLE:** This diagram shows the ages of my school teachers.
a) How many of the teachers are in their forties?
b) How old is the oldest teacher?

```
3 | 5
4 | 0 5 7 8
5 | 1 4 9
6 | 1 3
```
Key: 5 | 4 means 54

**ANSWER:**

Step 1: <u>WRITE DOWN ALL THE AGES</u> of the teachers, using the <u>key</u>.

Step 2: <u>ANSWER THE QUESTION</u>.

35,
40, 45, 47, 48,
51, 54, 59,
61, 63

a) four
b) 63

The key tells you <u>how to read</u> the diagram.
A 5 in the stem and a 4 in the leaf means 54.

## The Acid Test:
<u>LEARN</u> all the details from these <u>three</u> sections. <u>Turn over and write down everything you know.</u>

# Mean, Median, Mode and Range

If you don't manage to learn the 4 basic definitions below then you'll be passing up on some of the easiest marks in the whole Exam. It can't be *that* difficult can it?

**1) MODE        = MOST common**

Mode = most (emphasise the 'o' in each when you say them)

**2) MEDIAN        = MIDDLE value**

Median = mid (emphasise the m*d in each when you say them)

**3) MEAN        = TOTAL of items ÷ NUMBER of items**

Mean is just the average, "but it's mean 'cos you have to work it out"

**4) RANGE        = How far from the smallest to the biggest**

## THE GOLDEN RULE:

Mean, median, mode and range should be easy marks but even people who've gone to the incredible extent of learning them, still manage to lose marks in the Exam because they don't do this one vital step:

### Always REARRANGE the data in ASCENDING ORDER

(and check you have the same number of entries!)

**Example:**     *"Find the mean, median, mode and range of these numbers:"*

   *2, 5, 3, 2, 6, -4, 0, 9, -3, 1, 6, 3, -2, 3*        (14)

1) FIRST... rearrange them:        -4, -3, -2, 0, 1, 2, 2, 3, 3, 3, 5, 6, 6, 9        (✓14)

2) MEAN = $\dfrac{\text{total}}{\text{number}}$ = $\dfrac{-4-3-2+0+1+2+2+3+3+3+5+6+6+9}{14}$

   = 31 ÷ 14 = **2.21**

3) MEDIAN = the middle value (only when they're arranged in order of size, that is!).

When there are TWO MIDDLE NUMBERS, as in this case, then the median is HALFWAY BETWEEN THE TWO MIDDLE NUMBERS

   -4, -3, -2, 0, 1, 2, 2, 3, 3, 3, 5, 6, 6, 9
   ← seven numbers this side   ↑   seven numbers this side →
   Median = **2.5**

4) MODE = most common value, which is simply **3**. (Or you can say "The modal value is 3")

5) RANGE = distance from lowest to highest value, i.e. from -4 up to 9, = **13**

## The Acid Test:     LEARN The Four Definitions and THE GOLDEN RULE...

..then cover this page and write them down from memory.

1) Apply all that you have learnt to find the mean, median, mode and range for this set of data:    1, 3, 14, -5, 6, -12, 18, 7, 23, 10, -5, -14, 0, 25, 8

# Frequency Tables

Frequency Tables can either be done in <u>rows</u> or in <u>columns</u> of numbers, and they can be quite confusing, <u>but not if you learn these Eight Key Points</u>:

## Eight Key Points

1) <u>ALL FREQUENCY TABLES ARE THE SAME</u>.

2) The word <u>FREQUENCY</u> just means <u>HOW MANY</u>, so a frequency table is nothing more than a <u>"How many in each group"</u> table.

3) The <u>FIRST ROW</u> (or column) just gives the <u>GROUP LABELS</u>.

4) The <u>SECOND ROW</u> (or column) gives the <u>ACTUAL DATA</u>.

5) You have to <u>WORK OUT A THIRD ROW</u> (or column) <u>yourself</u>.

6) The <u>MEAN</u> is always found using:   **3rd Row total ÷ 2nd Row Total.**

7) The <u>MEDIAN</u> is found from the <u>MIDDLE VALUE</u> in the 2nd row.

8) The <u>RANGE</u> is found from <u>the EXTREMES of the first row</u>.

## Example

Here's a typical frequency table shown in both <u>ROW FORM</u> and <u>COLUMN FORM</u>:

| No. of Sisters | 0 | 1 | 2 | 3 | 4 | 5 | 6 |
|---|---|---|---|---|---|---|---|
| Frequency | 7 | 15 | 12 | 8 | 3 | 1 | 0 |

 **Row Form**

| No. of Sisters | Freq. |
|---|---|
| 0 | 7 |
| 1 | 15 |
| 2 | 12 |
| 3 | 8 |
| 4 | 3 |
| 5 | 1 |
| 6 | 0 |

**Column Form**

There's no real difference between these two forms, and you could get either one in your Exam. Whichever you get, make sure you remember these <u>THREE IMPORTANT FACTS</u>:

1) <u>THE 1ST ROW</u> (or column) gives us the <u>GROUP LABELS</u> for <u>the different categories</u>: i.e. "no sisters", "one sister", "two sisters", etc.

2) <u>THE 2ND ROW</u> (or column) <u>is the ACTUAL DATA</u> and tells us <u>HOW MANY (people)</u> <u>THERE ARE in each category</u> i.e. 7 people had "<u>no sisters</u>", 15 people had "<u>one sister</u>", etc.

3) <u>BUT YOU SHOULD SEE THE TABLE AS <i>UNFINISHED</i></u>, because it still needs a THIRD ROW (or column) and <u>TWO TOTALS</u> for the <u>2nd and 3rd rows</u> — see below:

This is what a (row form) table looks like when it's completed:

| No. of Sisters | 0 | 1 | 2 | 3 | 4 | 5 | 6 | Totals | |
|---|---|---|---|---|---|---|---|---|---|
| Frequency | 7 | 15 | 12 | 8 | 3 | 1 | 0 | 46 | (People asked) |
| No. × Freq. | 0 | 15 | 24 | 24 | 12 | 5 | 0 | 80 | (Sisters) |

"<u>Where does the third row come from?</u>"....I hear you cry!

<u>THE THIRD ROW</u> (or column) is <u>ALWAYS</u> obtained by <u>MULTIPLYING</u> the numbers <u>FROM THE FIRST 2 ROWS</u> (or columns).

**THIRD ROW = 1ST ROW × 2ND ROW**

*Once the table is complete, you can easily find the <u>MEAN, MEDIAN, MODE AND RANGE</u> (see P.65)*

## The Acid Test:

LEARN the <u>8 RULES</u> for Frequency Tables, then <u>turn over</u> and <u>write them down</u> to see what you know.

Using the methods you've just learnt, and this frequency table, find the MEAN, MEDIAN, MODE and RANGE of the no. of phones people have:

| No. of Phones | 0 | 1 | 2 | 3 | 4 | 5 | 6 |
|---|---|---|---|---|---|---|---|
| Frequency | 1 | 25 | 53 | 34 | 22 | 5 | 1 |

# Grouped Frequency Tables

These are a bit trickier than simple frequency tables, but they can still look deceptively simple, like this one which shows the distribution of weights of a bunch of 60 school kids.

| Weight (kg) | 31 — 40 | 41 — 50 | 51 — 60 | 61 — 70 | 71 — 80 |
|---|---|---|---|---|---|
| Frequency | 8 | 16 | 18 | 12 | 6 |

## Class Boundaries and Mid-Interval Values

*These are the two little jokers that make Grouped Frequency tables so tricky.*

1) THE CLASS BOUNDARIES are the precise values where you'd pass from one group into the next. For the above table the class boundaries would be at 40.5, 50.5, 60.5, etc. It's not difficult to work out what the class boundaries will be, just so long as you're clued up about it — they're nearly always "something.5" anyway, for obvious reasons.

2) THE MID-INTERVAL VALUES are pretty self-explanatory really and usually end up being "something.5" as well. Mind you a bit of care is needed to make sure you get the exact middle!

## "Estimating" the Mean using Mid-Interval Values

Just like with ordinary frequency tables you have to *add extra rows and find totals* to be able to work anything out. Also notice you can only "estimate" the mean from grouped data tables — you can't find it exactly unless you know all the original values.

> 1) Add a 3rd row and enter MID-INTERVAL VALUES for each group.
> 2) Add a 4th row and multiply FREQUENCY × MID-INTERVAL VALUE for each group.

| Weight (kg) | 31 — 40 | 41 — 50 | 51 — 60 | 61 — 70 | 71 — 80 | TOTALS |
|---|---|---|---|---|---|---|
| Frequency | 8 | 16 | 18 | 12 | 6 | 60 |
| Mid-Interval Value | 35.5 | 45.5 | 55.5 | 65.5 | 75.5 | — |
| Frequency × Mid-Interval Value | 284 | 728 | 999 | 786 | 453 | 3250 |

1) ESTIMATING THE MEAN is then the usual thing of DIVIDING THE TOTALS:

$$\text{Mean} = \frac{\text{Overall Total (Final Row)}}{\text{Frequency Total (2nd Row)}} = \frac{3250}{60} = \underline{54.2}$$

2) THE MODE is still nice'n'easy: the modal group is 51 — 60kg (the one with the most entries).

3) THE MEDIAN can't be found exactly but you can at least say which group it's in. If all the data were put in order, the 30th/31st entries would be in the 51 — 60kg group.

## The Acid Test:

LEARN all the details on this page, then turn over and write down everything you've learned. Good clean fun.

1) Estimate the mean for this table:
2) Also state the modal group and the approximate value of the median.

| Length(cm) | 15.5 — | 16.5 — | 17.5 — | 18.5 — 19.5 |
|---|---|---|---|---|
| Frequency | 12 | 18 | 23 | 8 |

# Cumulative Frequency Tables

Usually you'll get a half-finished table and they'll ask you to complete it as a cumulative frequency table. This means adding a third row and filling it in (as shown in the example below). Make sure you know these:

## FOUR KEY POINTS

1) __CUMULATIVE FREQUENCY__ just means __ADDING IT UP AS YOU GO ALONG__.
So each entry in the table for cumulative frequency is just "__THE TOTAL SO FAR__".

2) You have to __ADD A THIRD ROW__ to the table
— this is just the __RUNNING TOTAL__ of the 2nd row.

3) If you're plotting a graph, always plot points using the __HIGHEST VALUE__ in each group (of row 1) with the value from __row 3__. (i.e. plot at the _class boundaries_) i.e. for the example below, plot 13 at _160.5_, 33 at _170.5_, etc.

4) __CUMULATIVE FREQUENCY__ is always plotted up the side of a graph, not across.

## Example

_"Complete the table below for cumulative frequency:"_

| Height (cm) | 141 – 150 | 151 – 160 | 161 – 170 | 171 – 180 | 181 – 190 | 191 – 200 | 201 – 210 |
|---|---|---|---|---|---|---|---|
| Frequency | 4 | 9 | 20 | 33 | 36 | 15 | 3 |

__ANSWER:__ _Add in the third row_ where each entry for row 3 (cumulative frequency) is just "__THE TOTAL SO FAR__" of the numbers for frequency (row 2).

| Height (cm) | 141 – 150 | 151 – 160 | 161 – 170 | 171 – 180 | 181 – 190 | 191 – 200 | 201 – 210 |
|---|---|---|---|---|---|---|---|
| Frequency | 4 | 9 | 20 | 33 | 36 | 15 | 3 |
| Cumulative Frequency | 4 (AT 150.5) | 13 (AT 160.5) | 33 (AT 170.5) | 66 (AT 180.5) | 102 (AT 190.5) | 117 (AT 200.5) | 120 (AT 210.5) |

The graph is plotted from these pairs: (150.5, 4) (160.5, 13) (170.5, 33) (180.5, 66) etc. because the cumulative frequency has only reached those values (4, 13, 33 etc.) by the TOP END of each group, not at the middle of each group, and _150.5_ is the actual _CLASS BOUNDARY_ between the first group and the next — a tricky detail.

## The Acid Test:

__LEARN__ the 4 Key Points, then __turn over__ and __write them down__.

Complete the table shown here for cumulative frequency.

| Weight (kg) | 41 – 45 | 46 – 50 | 51 – 55 | 56 – 60 | 61 – 65 | 66 – 70 | 71 – 75 |
|---|---|---|---|---|---|---|---|
| Frequency | 2 | 7 | 17 | 25 | 19 | 8 | 2 |

# The Cumulative Frequency Curve

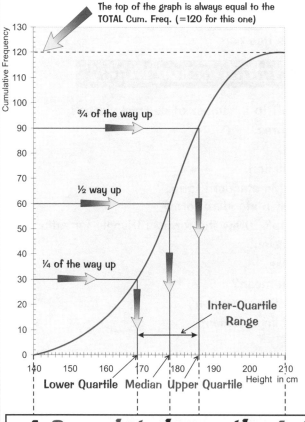

The top of the graph is always equal to the TOTAL Cum. Freq. (=120 for this one)

¾ of the way up

½ way up

¼ of the way up

Inter-Quartile Range

Lower Quartile   Median   Upper Quartile   Height in cm

*From the cumulative frequency curve* you can get THREE VITAL STATISTICS:

1) **MEDIAN**
   *Exactly halfway UP*, then across, then down and *read off the bottom scale.*

2) **LOWER AND UPPER QUARTILES**
   *Exactly ¼ and ¾ UP the side*, then across, then down and *read off the bottom scale.*

3) **THE INTER-QUARTILE RANGE**
   The distance *on the bottom scale* between the lower and upper quartiles.

So from the above cumulative frequency curve, we can easily get these results:

MEDIAN = <u>178cm</u>
LOWER QUARTILE = <u>169cm</u>
UPPER QUARTILE = <u>186cm</u>
INTER-QUARTILE RANGE = <u>17cm</u>   (186-169)

## A Box plot shows the Inter-Quartile Range as a Box

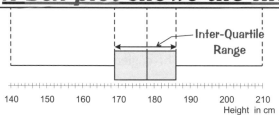

Inter-Quartile Range

140   150   160   170   180   190   200   210
Height in cm

**TO CREATE YOUR VERY OWN BOX PLOT:**
1) *Draw the scale* along the bottom.
2) *Draw a box* the length of the *inter-quartile range.*
3) *Draw a line* down the box to show the *median.*
4) *Draw "whiskers"* up to the *maximum and minimum.*

(They're sometimes called "Box and Whisker diagrams".)

## Interpreting The shape

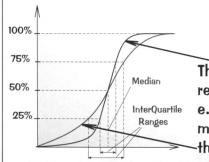

100%

75%

50%

25%

Median

InterQuartile Ranges

The shape of a <u>CUMULATIVE FREQUENCY CURVE</u> also tells you *how spread out* the data values are.

This 'tighter' distribution (which has a small interquartile range) represents very CONSISTENT results, which is usually good — e.g. *lifetimes of batteries or light bulbs* all very close together means a *good product*, compared to the other curve where the lifetimes show *wide variation*, i.e. poor quality product.

## The Acid Test:

<u>LEARN THIS PAGE</u>, then <u>cover it up</u> and <u>write down all the important details.</u>

Using your completed frequency table from the previous page, draw the cumulative frequency graph and box plot and use them to find the three vital statistics.

# Revision Test for Stage Two

More difficult questions, *but just keep reminding yourself that they're the very best revision you can do.* These questions are all very plain and very straightforward. They just test whether or not you've actually *learnt* all the *basic facts* in Stage Two. It's really important to keep practising these as often as you can.

## Keep learning these basic facts until you know them

1) What are the three steps in the method for rounding off to a number of decimal places?
2) Describe how you round to a number of significant figures.
3) State three rules for deciding on appropriate accuracy.
4) Explain how you would estimate the answer to a calculation.
5) Write down the general format for a number expressed in standard form.
   What are the three basic rules for expressing a number in standard form?
6) Which two alternative forms can a ratio be converted to?  Draw the formula triangle for ratios.
7) Write down the three-step method for proportional division.
8) List the six steps of the method for rearranging formulas.
9) What are the four inequality symbols and what do they mean?
10) What are the rules of algebra for inequalities?  What's the exception?
11) List the four steps for solving an equation using trial and improvement.
12) What is the formula for gradient?
13) Write down the method for finding a gradient.
14) What's the easiest method for sketching the graph of an equation?
15) Detail the six steps for plotting a graph using $y = mx + c$.
16) Sketch the graph of $y = x^2$.
17) Detail a safe method for filling in a table of values.
18) How do you determine the meaning of the gradient of a graph?
19) Write the formula for Pythagoras' Theorem.
20) Draw out three formula triangles to find $\sin\theta$, $\cos\theta$ and $\tan\theta$ for a right-angled triangle.
21) List the first three rules of circle geometry.
22) What two facts must you specify for an enlargement?  Describe the method for drawing one.
23) Draw out the formula triangles for density and speed.
24) Write the formula for the area of a:
   a) rectangle,  b) triangle,  c) circle.
25) Write the formula for the volume of a:
   a) general prism,  b) triangular prism,  c) cylinder.
26) List the three steps of the method for converting angles on a pie chart back to the original data.
27) On a scatter graph, what does correlation mean?  Draw a graph with:
   a) strong positive correlation,  b) moderate negative correlation,  c) zero correlation
28) Draw an example of a stem and leaf diagram and explain what it means.
29) Give the definitions for mean, median, mode and range.
30) What are the eight key points for frequency tables?
31) How do you work out the mean, median, mode and range from a frequency table?
32) How can you estimate the mean from a grouped frequency table?
33) Describe a cumulative frequency table.  How is it different from a frequency table?
34) Sketch a typical cumulative frequency graph.
35) What four statistics can you get from a cumulative frequency graph?  How do you obtain them?

# Powers (or "Indices")

Powers are a very useful shorthand:

$$2\times2\times2\times2\times2\times2\times2 = 2^7 \text{ ("two to the power 7")}$$
$$4\times4\times4 = 4^3 \text{ ("four cubed")}$$

That bit is easy to remember. Unfortunately, there are <u>EIGHT SPECIAL RULES</u> for Powers that are not quite so easy, but <u>*you do need to know them for the Exam*</u>:

## The Eight Rules

**1)** When <u>MULTIPLYING</u>, you <u>ADD</u> the powers.

e.g. $3^4 \times 3^6 = 3^{6+4} = 3^{10}$ $\qquad 8^3 \times 8^5 = 8^{3+5} = 8^8$

**2)** When <u>DIVIDING</u>, you <u>SUBTRACT</u> the powers.

e.g. $5^4 \div 5^2 = 5^{4-2} = 5^2$ $\qquad 12^8/12^3 = 12^{8-3} = 12^5$

**3)** When <u>RAISING</u> one power to another, you <u>MULTIPLY</u> the powers.

e.g. $(3^2)^4 = 3^{2\times4} = 3^8,$ $\qquad (5^4)^6 = 5^{24}$

**4)** <u>$X^1 = X$,</u> <u>ANYTHING TO THE POWER 1 is just ITSELF.</u>

e.g. $3^1 = 3, \quad 6 \times 6^3 = 6^4, \quad 4^3 \div 4^2 = 4^{3-2} = 4^1 = 4$

**5)** <u>$X^0 = 1$,</u> <u>ANYTHING TO THE POWER 0 is just 1.</u>

e.g. $5^0 = 1 \qquad 67^0 = 1 \qquad 3^4/3^4 = 3^{4-4} = 3^0 = 1$

**6)** <u>$1^x = 1$,</u> <u>1 TO ANY POWER is still just 1.</u>

e.g. $1^{23} = 1 \qquad 1^{89} = 1 \qquad 1^2 = 1 \qquad 1^{1012} = 1$

**7)** <u>FRACTIONAL POWERS</u> mean one thing: <u>ROOTS.</u>

The power ½ means <u>*square root*</u>, e.g. $25^{\frac{1}{2}} = \sqrt{25} = 5$
The power ⅓ means <u>*cube root*</u>, e.g. $64^{\frac{1}{3}} = \sqrt[3]{64} = 4$

**8)** <u>NEGATIVE POWERS</u> — Turn it UPSIDE-DOWN.

$X^{-1} = 1/X$. This is called the <u>*reciprocal*</u> of **X**. To find 1/X for any number, make **X** into a fraction and turn it upside-down. *(0 has NO reciprocal, because you can't divide by 0)*
<u>IN GENERAL, when you have a negative power, turn the number the other way up and make the power positive, LIKE THIS:</u>

e.g. $7^{-2} = \dfrac{1}{7^2} = \dfrac{1}{49}$ $\qquad \left(\dfrac{3}{5}\right)^{-2} = \left(\dfrac{5}{3}\right)^{+2} = \dfrac{5^2}{3^2} = \dfrac{25}{9}$

## The Acid Test:

LEARN the <u>Eight Rules</u> for Powers. Then <u>turn over</u> and <u>write it all down</u>. Keep trying until you can do it!

Then cover the page and apply the rules to <u>SIMPLIFY</u> these:
1) a) $3^2 \times 3^6$   b) $4^3 \div 4^2$   c) $(8^3)^4$   d) $(3^2 \times 3^3 \times 1^6)/3^5$   e) $7^3 \times 7 \times 7^2$
2) a) $5^2 \times 5^7 \times 5^3$   b) $1^3 \times 5^0 \times 6^2$   c) $(4^3 \times 4 \times 4^{-2}) \div (2^3 \times 2^4)$

# Compound Growth and Decay

This can also be called "Exponential" Growth or Decay. But you don't want to know that. You want to know this:

## The Formula

This topic is simple if you LEARN THIS FORMULA. If you don't, it's pretty well impossible:

$$N = N_0\left(1 + \frac{r}{100}\right)^n$$

Existing amount at this time

Initial amount

Percentage change per day/hour/year

Number of days/hrs/yrs

## Percentage Increase and Decrease

The $(1 + r/100)$ bit might look a bit confusing in the formula but in practice it's really easy:

E.g.   5% increase will be 1.05          5% decrease will be 0.95    (= 1 − 0.05)
          26% increase will be 1.26        26% decrease will be 0.74    (= 1 − 0.26)

You can also combine increases and decreases:

E.g.   A 20% increase in value **a** followed by a 20% decrease will be $0.8 \times 1.2 \times$ **a**.
          They <u>don't</u> cancel each other out.

## 3 Examples to show you how EASY it is:

**1)**  *"A man invests £1000 in a savings account which pays 8% per annum. How much will there be after 6 years?"*  *(This is known as compound interest.)*

ANSWER: Usual formula (as above):          Amount $= 1000 \times (1.08)^6 = £1586.87$

                                                                        Initial amount   8% increase   6 years

**2)**  *"The activity of a radio-isotope falls by 12% every hour. If the initial activity is 800 counts per minute, what will it be after 7 hours?"*

ANSWER: Same old formula:

$$\text{Activity} = \text{Initial value}(1 - 12/100)^n$$

$$\text{Activity} = 800(1 - 0.12)^7 = 800 \times (0.88)^7 = \underline{327 \text{ cpm}}$$

**3)**  *"In a sample of bacteria, there are initially 500 cells and they increase in number by 15% each day. Find the formula relating the number of cells, n, and the number of days, d."*

ANSWER: Well stone me, it's the same old easy-peasy compound increase formula <u>again</u>:

$$n = n_0(1 + 0.15)^d \quad \text{or finished off:} \quad \underline{n = 500 \times (1.15)^d}$$

## The Acid Test:

LEARN THE FORMULA. Also learn the 3 Examples. Then <u>turn over and write it all down</u>.

1) The population of a colony of stick insects increases by 4% per week. Initially there are 30. How many will there be after 12 weeks?

2) The speed of a tennis ball rolled along a smooth floor falls by 16% every second. If the initial speed was 5m/s find the speed after 20 seconds.

# Irrational Numbers, Surds and D.O.T.S.

<u>RATIONAL NUMBERS</u> The vast majority of numbers are rational. They are always either:

> 1) A whole number (either positive (+ve), or negative (–ve))   e.g.  4,  -5,  -12
> 2) A fraction p/q,  where p and q are whole numbers (+ve or –ve). e.g. ¼, -½, ¾
> 3) A finite or repeating decimal, e.g.  0.125  0.3333333333...   0.143143143143..

<u>IRRATIONAL NUMBERS</u> are messy!

> 1) They are always <u>NEVER-ENDING NON-REPEATING DECIMALS</u>. $\pi$ is irrational.
> 2) A *good source* of <u>IRRATIONAL NUMBERS</u> is <u>SQUARE ROOTS AND CUBE ROOTS</u>.

## *Manipulating Surds*

*It sounds like something to do with controlling difficult children, but it isn't. Surds are expressions with irrational square roots in them. You <u>MUST USE THEM</u> if they ask you for an <u>EXACT</u> answer. There are a few simple rules to learn:*

1) $\sqrt{a} \times \sqrt{b} = \sqrt{ab}$   e.g. $\sqrt{2} \times \sqrt{3} = \sqrt{2 \times 3} = \sqrt{6}$     — also $\sqrt{b}^2 = b$, fairly obviously

2) $\dfrac{\sqrt{a}}{\sqrt{b}} = \sqrt{\dfrac{a}{b}}$     e.g. $\dfrac{\sqrt{8}}{\sqrt{2}} = \sqrt{\dfrac{8}{2}} = \sqrt{4} = 2$

3) $\sqrt{a} + \sqrt{b}$ — <u>NOTHING DOING</u>...   (in other words it is definitely NOT $\sqrt{a+b}$ )

4) $(a + \sqrt{b})^2 = (a + \sqrt{b})(a + \sqrt{b}) = a^2 + 2a\sqrt{b} + b$  ( NOT just $a^2 + \sqrt{b}^2$ )

5) $(a + \sqrt{b})(a - \sqrt{b}) = a^2 + a\sqrt{b} - a\sqrt{b} - \sqrt{b}^2 = a^2 - b$

6) Express $\dfrac{3}{\sqrt{5}}$ in the form $\dfrac{a\sqrt{5}}{b}$ where a and b are whole numbers.

> To do this you must *"<u>RATIONALISE the denominator</u>"*, which just means multiplying top and bottom by $\sqrt{5}$: $\dfrac{3\sqrt{5}}{\sqrt{5}\sqrt{5}} = \dfrac{3\sqrt{5}}{5}$   so a = 3 and b = 5

7) If you want an *exact* answer, <u>LEAVE THE SURDS IN</u>. As soon as you go using that calculator, you'll get a *big fat rounding error* — and the <u>WRONG</u> answer. Don't say I didn't warn you...

## <u>D.O.T.S.</u> — *The Difference Of Two Squares:*

$$\underline{a^2 - b^2 = (a + b)(a - b)}$$

The "difference of two squares" (D.O.T.S. for short) is where you have "one thing squared" take away "another thing squared". In the Exam you'll more than likely be asked to factorise a D.O.T.S. expression (i.e. put it into two brackets as above). Too many people have more trouble than they should with this. Make sure you <u>LEARN</u> how to do these three important examples:

1) Factorise $9P^2 - 16Q^2$.     Answer:  $9P^2 - 16Q^2 = \underline{(3P + 4Q)(3P - 4Q)}$
2) Factorise $1 - T^4$ .     Answer:  $1 - T^4 = \underline{(1 + T^2)(1 - T^2)}$
3) Factorise $3K^2 - 75H^2$.   Answer:  $3K^2 - 75H^2 = 3(K^2 - 25H^2) = \underline{3(K + 5H)(K - 5H)}$

## *The Acid Test:*     LEARN the 7 rules for manipulating surds, then <u>turn over</u> and <u>write them all down</u>.

1) Simplify a) $\left(1+\sqrt{2}\right)^2 - \left(1-\sqrt{2}\right)^2$     b) $\left(1+\sqrt{2}\right)^2 - \left(2\sqrt{2}-\sqrt{2}\right)^2$

2) Factorise  a) $4s^4 - 9t^2$     b) $2p^2 - 32q^2r^2$

# Simultaneous Equations

These are OK as long as you learn these <u>SIX STEPS</u> in every meticulous detail.

## There are Six Steps in the Solution

We'll use these two equations for this example:     $2x = 6 - 4y$   and   $-3 - 3y = 4x$

**1) <u>REARRANGE BOTH EQUATIONS INTO THE FORM</u>:**     <u>ax + by = c</u>
where a,b,c are numbers,     (which can be negative).
Also <u>LABEL THE TWO EQUATIONS</u>   —① and   —②

$2x + 4y = 6$          —①
$-4x - 3y = 3$          —②

**2) You need to <u>MATCH UP THE NUMBERS IN FRONT</u> (the "coefficients")**
of either the x's or y's in <u>BOTH EQUATIONS</u>.
To do this you may need to <u>MULTIPLY</u> one or both equations by a
suitable number. You should then <u>RELABEL</u> them: —③ and —④

①×2 :  $4x + 8y = 12$        —③        (This gives us +4x in equation —③ to match
        $-4x - 3y = 3$        —④        the −4x in equation —②, now called —④)

**3) <u>ADD OR SUBTRACT THE TWO EQUATIONS</u> ...**
...to eliminate the terms with the same coefficient.
If the <u>coefficients are the SAME</u> ( both +ve or both −ve) then <u>SUBTRACT</u>.
If the <u>coefficients are OPPOSITE</u> ( one +ve and one −ve) then <u>ADD</u>.

③+④    $0x + 5y = 15$        (In this case we have +4x and −4x so we ADD)

**4) <u>SOLVE THE RESULTING EQUATION</u> to find whichever letter is left in it.**

$5y = 15 \Rightarrow \underline{y = 3}$

**5) <u>SUB THIS BACK</u> into equation ① and solve it to find the other quantity.**

Sub in ①:     $2x + 4 \times 3 = 6 \Rightarrow 2x + 12 = 6 \Rightarrow 2x = -6 \Rightarrow \underline{x = -3}$

**6) Then <u>SUBSTITUTE BOTH THESE VALUES INTO EQUATION</u> ② to make**
sure it works out properly.  If it doesn't then you've done
something wrong and you'll have to do it all again!

Sub x and y in ②:   $-4 \times -3 - 3 \times 3 = 12 - 9 = \underline{3}$
                which is right, so it's worked.

So the solutions are:   <u>x = -3</u>,  <u>y = 3</u>

## The Acid Test: LEARN the _6 Steps_ for solving _Simultaneous Equations_.

Remember, you only know them when you can write them all out from memory, so
turn over the page and try it.  Then apply the 6 steps to find F and G given that
$2F - 10 = 4G$     and     $3G = 4F - 15$

# Simultaneous Equations with Graphs

On the opposite page is the *tricky algebra method* for solving simultaneous equations.
On this page is the *nice easy graph method* for solving them.
You could be asked to do *either* method in the Exam so make sure you *learn them both*.

## Solving Simultaneous Equations Using Graphs

This is a very easy way to find the x- and y- solutions to two simultaneous equations.
Here's the simple rule:

> **THE SOLUTION** OF TWO **SIMULTANEOUS EQUATIONS** IS SIMPLY
> THE **X** AND **Y** VALUES <u>**WHERE THEIR GRAPHS CROSS**</u>

### Three Step Method

1) Do a <u>*"TABLE OF 3 VALUES"*</u> for both equations.

2) Draw the Two <u>*GRAPHS*</u>.

3) Find the X- and Y-values <u>*WHERE THEY CROSS*</u>.

*Easy Peasy.*

### Example

*"Draw the graphs for "Y = 2X + 3" and "Y = 6 – 4X" and then use your graphs to solve them."*

1) <u>TABLE OF 3 VALUES</u> (see P.51)
    for both equations:

| X | 0 | 2 | -2 |
|---|---|---|---|
| Y | 3 | 7 | -1 |

| X | 0 | 2 | 3 |
|---|---|---|---|
| Y | 6 | -2 | -6 |

2) <u>DRAW THE GRAPHS:</u>

3) <u>WHERE THEY CROSS,</u>
      x = ½, y = 4.
      And that's the answer!

> x = ½ and y = 4

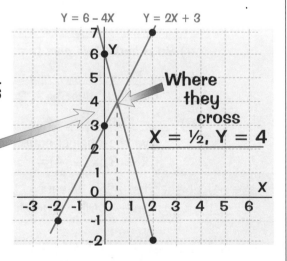

Y = 6 – 4X      Y = 2X + 3

Where they cross
X = ½, Y = 4

## The Acid Test:

<u>LEARN</u> the Simple Rule and the <u>3 step method</u> for <u>solving simultaneous equations</u> using <u>GRAPHS</u>.

1) Cover the page and write down the Simple Rule and the 3 step method.
2) Use graphs to find the solutions to these pairs of equations:
   a)  y = 4x – 4  and  y = 6 – x          b) y = 2x    and   y = 6 – 2x

# Quadratics

## Factorising a Quadratic

*"Factorising a quadratic"* means *"putting it into 2 brackets"* — you'll need to remember that. There are several different methods for doing this, so stick with the one you're happiest with. If you have no preference then learn this one. The standard format for any quadratic equations is:

$$x^2 + bx + c = 0$$   (e.g. $x^2 + 3x + 2 = 0$)

## Factorising Method

1) ALWAYS rearrange into the STANDARD FORMAT: $x^2 + bx + c = 0$.

2) Write down the TWO BRACKETS with the x's in: $(x \quad )(x \quad )=0$.

3) Then find 2 numbers that MULTIPLY to give "c" (the end number) but also ADD/SUBTRACT to give "b" (the coefficient of x).

4) Put them in and check that the +/− signs work out properly.

## Example

*"Solve $x^2 - x = 12$ by factorising."*

ANSWER: 1) First rearrange it (into the standard format):   $x^2 - x - 12 = 0$

2) The initial brackets are (as ever):   $(x \quad )(x \quad )=0$

3) We now want to look at all pairs of numbers that multiply to give "c" (=12), but which also add or subtract to give the value of b: (-1)

| | | |
|---|---|---|
| $1 \times 12$ | Add/subtract to give: | 13 or 11 |
| $2 \times 6$ | Add/subtract to give: | 8 or 4    this is what we're after |
| $3 \times 4$ | Add/subtract to give: | 7 or ①← (1 is "b", within ±) |

4) So 3 and 4 will give b = ±1, so put them in:   $(x \quad 3)(x \quad 4)=0$

5) Now fill in the +/− signs so that the 3 and 4 add/subtract to give -1 (=b), Clearly it must be +3 and − 4 so we'll have:   $(x + 3)(x - 4)=0$

6) As an ESSENTIAL check, EXPAND the brackets out again to make sure they give the original equation:
$(x + 3)(x - 4)= x^2 + 3x - 4x - 12= x^2 - x - 12$

We're not finished yet mind, because $(x + 3)(x - 4)=0$ is only the factorised form of the equation — we have yet to give the actual SOLUTIONS. This is very easy:

7) THE SOLUTIONS are simply the two numbers in the brackets, but with OPPOSITE +/− SIGNS: i.e.   $x = -3$ or $+4$

*Make sure you remember that last step. It's the difference between SOLVING THE EQUATION and merely factorising it.*

## The Acid Test: LEARN the 7 steps for solving quadratics by factorising.

1) Solve these by the factor method:   a) $x^2 + 5x + 6 = 0$   b) $x^2 + 8x + 12 = 0$
c) $x^2 + 5x - 24 = 0$   d) $x^2 - 6x + 9 = 16$

# Four Graphs You Should Recognise

## 1) Straight Line Graphs: "y = mx + c"

Straight line equations are really quite easy to spot — they have an _x-term_, a _y-term_ and _a number_ and that's it. There's no $x^2$ or $x^3$ terms or any other fancy things.
(You should have covered this in Stage 2, so make sure you know it — P50-P52.)

EXAMPLES:

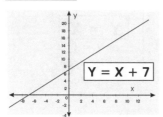

Y = X + 7

| Straight lines | | Rearranged into "y = mx + c" | |
|---|---|---|---|
| $y = 2 + 3x$ | $\rightarrow$ | $y = 3x + 2$ | (m=3, c=2) |
| $2y - 4x = 7$ | $\rightarrow$ | $y = 2x + 3\frac{1}{2}$ | (m=2, c=3½) |
| $x - y = 0$ | $\rightarrow$ | $y = x + 0$ | (m=1, c=0) |
| $4x - 3 = 5y$ | $\rightarrow$ | $y = 0.8x - 0.6$ | (m=0.8, c=0.6) |
| $3y + 3x = 12$ | $\rightarrow$ | $y = -x + 4$ | (m=-1, c=4) |

## 2) Quadratic Graphs: "$x^2$"

$$y = ax^2 + bx + c$$

All $x^2$ graphs have the same SYMMETRICAL "U" shape:

If the "a" is positive then the graph makes a "u", but if the $x^2$ part has a "<u>minus</u>" in front of it (e.g. $-x^2$) then the "u" is <u>upside down</u> — making it an "n" shape.
(Remember — "n" = "negative.")

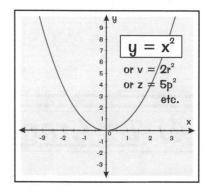

$y = x^2$
or $v = 2r^2$
or $z = 5p^2$
etc.

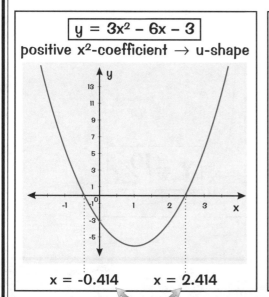

$y = 3x^2 - 6x - 3$
positive $x^2$-coefficient $\rightarrow$ u-shape

x = -0.414        x = 2.414

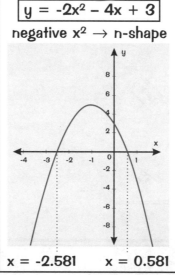

$y = -2x^2 - 4x + 3$
negative $x^2 \rightarrow$ n-shape

x = -2.581        x = 0.581

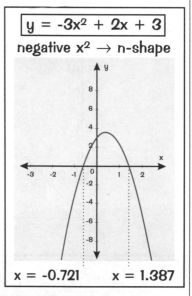

$y = -3x^2 + 2x + 3$
negative $x^2 \rightarrow$ n-shape

x = -0.721        x = 1.387

The **_SOLUTIONS_** or **_ROOTS_** of the quadratic equation are the points or point where the $x^2$ graph crosses the <u>x-AXIS</u>.

# Four Graphs You Should Recognise

## 3) X³ Graphs:

Y = "something with X³ in it"

All X³ graphs have the same basic _wiggle_ in the middle, but it can be a flat wiggle or a more pronounced wiggle.

Notice that "_–X³ graphs_" always come _down from top left_ whereas the _+X³_ ones go _up from bottom left_.

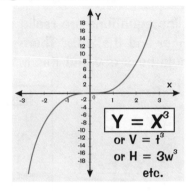

Y = X³
or V = t³
or H = 3w³
etc.

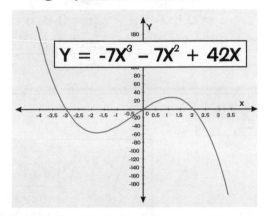

Y = -7X³ – 7X² + 42X

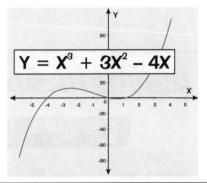

Y = X³ + 3X² – 4X

## 4) 1/x Graphs:

Y = ^A⁄x , where A is some number.

These graphs are _all the same shape_, the only difference being how close in they get at the corner. They are all _symmetrical about the line y=x_. This is also the graph you get when x and y are in _inverse proportion_.

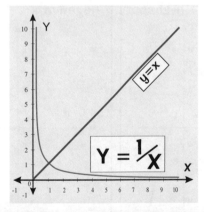

y=x

Y = ¹⁄X

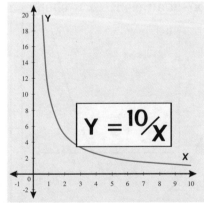

Y = ¹⁰⁄X

## The Acid Test:

LEARN all the details about the _4 Types of Graph_, their equations and their shapes.

Then _turn over_ and _sketch three examples_ of each of the _four types_ of graph — and if you can also give some extra details about their equations, _so much the better_. Remember, if you don't _LEARN IT_, then it's a waste of time even reading it. This is true for all revision.

# Circle Geometry

You'll have to learn these if you want to be able to do circle problems.

## 1) ANGLE IN A SEMICIRCLE = 90°

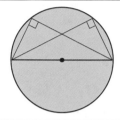

A triangle drawn from the <u>two ends of a diameter</u> will **ALWAYS** make an <u>angle of 90° where it hits</u> the edge of the circle, no matter where it hits.

## 2) CHORD BISECTOR IS A DIAMETER

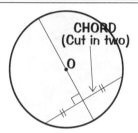

A CHORD is any line <u>drawn across a circle</u>, and no matter where you draw a chord, the line that <u>cuts it exactly in half</u> (at 90°), will go <u>through the centre of the circle</u> and so it'll <u>have to be</u> a *DIAMETER*.

## 3) ANGLES IN THE SAME SEGMENT ARE EQUAL

All triangles drawn from a chord will have <u>the same angle where they touch the circle.</u>

Also, the two angles on opposite sides of the chord <u>add up to 180°</u>.

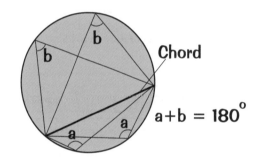

$a+b = 180^{o}$

When the chord chops the circle in half (to form 2 <u>semicircles</u>), the angle at the edge of the circle is <u>always a right angle</u> (see above).

## 4) ANGLE AT THE CENTRE IS TWICE THE ANGLE AT THE EDGE

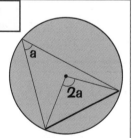

The angle subtended at the centre of a circle is <u>EXACTLY DOUBLE</u> the angle subtended at the edge of the circle from the same two points (two ends of the same chord). The phrase "<u>angle subtended at</u>" is nothing complicated, it's just a bit posher than saying "<u>angle made at</u>".

## 5) OPPOSITE ANGLES OF A CYCLIC QUADRILATERAL ADD UP TO 180°

<u>a+c=180°</u>
<u>b+d=180°</u>

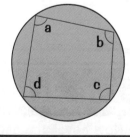

A *cyclic quadrilateral* is a <u>4-sided shape with every corner touching the circle</u>. Each pair of opposite angles add up to 180°.

## The Acid Test:

LEARN all <u>Five Rules</u> on this page.
Then <u>turn over and write them all down</u>.

Check your effort and try again — and keep trying till you can do it!

# Projections, Congruence and Similarity

## Projections *show* the Scale of the Shape

A '*projection*' shows the relative size and shape of an object from either the *front*, *side* or *back* — they're usually known as '*elevations*'. A '*plan*' shows the view from *above*. They're always *drawn to scale*.

**FRONT Elevation**

— the view you'd see if you looked from directly *in front*:

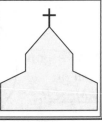

**SIDE Elevation**

— the view you'd see if you looked from directly to *one side*:

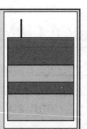

**PLAN**

— the view you'd see if you looked from directly *above*:

If they're feeling really mean (and they often are), you might get a question on:

This one's a bit trickier, so you might want to spend a little longer practising it — just to get your head round it.

**ISOMETRIC Projection**

— this is where the shape is drawn (again, to scale) from a view at *equal angles to* all three axes (*x, y and z*). Or more simply, it's a drawing like this:

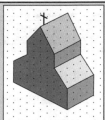

## Congruence *and* Similarity

*Congruence* is another ridiculous maths word which sounds really complicated when it's not: If two shapes are *CONGRUENT*, they're simply *the same* — *the same size and the same shape*.

### CONGRUENT

— same size, same shape

A, B, and C are *CONGRUENT* (with each other)

### SIMILAR

— same shape, *different size*

D and E are *SIMILAR*, (but not congruent)

Remember: when you have *similar* shapes *the angles are always the same*.

## The Acid Test:
Make sure you understand **ALL FOUR TYPES OF PROJECTION**, and **LEARN** exactly what "**SIMILAR**" and "**CONGRUENT**" mean.

Now cover the page and write down what you've learned. Then **REMEMBER** it forever!

1) Draw plan, front and side elevations and an isometric projection of your own house.

2) a) Which of these four shapes are similar?
   b) Which are congruent?

i)  ii)  iii)  iv)

# Length, Area and Volume

## Identifying Formulas Just by Looking at Them

(The proper name for this is "dimensional analysis". Remember that — it might be in the exam.)

This isn't as bad as it sounds, since we're only talking about the formulas for 3 things:

### LENGTH, AREA and VOLUME

The rules are as simple as this:

**AREA FORMULAS** always have **LENGTHS MULTIPLIED IN PAIRS**

**VOLUME FORMULAS** always have **LENGTHS MULTIPLIED IN GROUPS OF THREE**

**LENGTH FORMULAS** (such as perimeter) always have **LENGTHS OCCURRING SINGLY**

In formulas of course, LENGTHS ARE REPRESENTED BY LETTERS, so when you look at a formula you're looking for:

GROUPS OF LETTERS MULTIPLIED TOGETHER in *ONES*, *TWOS* or *THREES*.

BUT REMEMBER, $\pi$ is NOT a length.

### Examples:

| | | |
|---|---|---|
| $4\pi r^2 + 6d^2$ (area) | $Lwh + 6r^2L$ (volume) | ($r^2$ means r × r, |
| $4\pi r + 15L$ (length) | $6hp + \pi r^2 + 7h^2$ (area) | don't forget) |
| $5p^2L - 4k^3/7$ (volume) | $2\pi d - 14r/3$ (length) | |

Watch out for these last two tricky ones:   (Why are they tricky?)

$3p(2b + a)$     (area)         $3\pi h(L^2 + 4P^2)$ (volume)

## Converting Between Different Units of Volume

A lot of people mess this up in the exam and lose marks. It's not difficult if you take the time to SIT DOWN AND LEARN IT.

**MEMORISE THESE CONVERSION FACTORS:**

$1\,cm^3 = 1000\,mm^3 = 1 \times 10^3\,mm^3$

$1\,m^3 = 1\,000\,000\,cm^3 = 1 \times 10^6\,cm^3$

$1\,m^3 = 1\,000\,000\,000\,mm^3 = 1 \times 10^9\,mm^3$

Make sure you learn these as ordinary numbers AND in standard form (see P.43). If you need reminding about "Conversion Factors", look back at P.34.

## The Acid Test:
LEARN the Rules for Identifying Formulas and Converting Volumes. Turn over and write it all down.

1) Identify each of these expressions as an area, volume, or perimeter:
   $\pi r^2$,   $Lwh$,   $\pi d$,   $\frac{1}{2}bh$,   $2bh + 4lp$,   $4r^2p + 3\pi d^3$,   $2\pi r(3L + 5T)$
2) Convert these to $m^3$ (write your answers in standard form): $6500cm^3$,   $76\,800mm^3$

# Solids and Nets

You need to know what _Face_, _Edge_ and _Vertex_ mean:

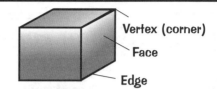

Vertex (corner)

Face

Edge

## Surface Area and Nets

1) <u>SURFACE AREA</u> only applies to solid 3-D objects, and it's simply _the total area of all the outer surfaces added together_. If you were painting it, it's all the bits you'd paint!

2) There is <u>never a simple formula</u> for surface area — _you have to work out each side in turn and then_ <u>ADD THEM ALL TOGETHER</u>.

3) <u>A NET</u> is just <u>A SOLID SHAPE FOLDED OUT FLAT</u>.

4) So obviously: <u>SURFACE AREA OF SOLID = AREA OF NET</u>.

There are 4 nets that you need to know really well for the Exam, and they're shown below. They may well ask you to draw one of these nets and then work out its area.

### 1) _Triangular Prism_

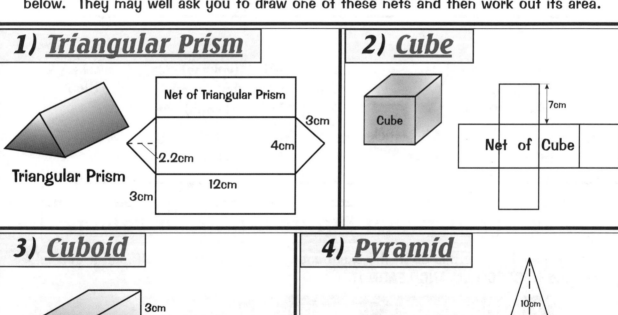

Net of Triangular Prism

3cm

4cm

2.2cm

12cm

3cm

**Triangular Prism**

### 2) _Cube_

Cube

7cm

Net of Cube

### 3) _Cuboid_

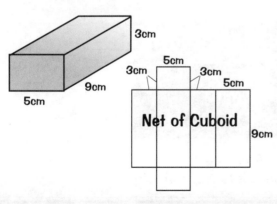

3cm

5cm

3cm     3cm

3cm     5cm

9cm

5cm

**Net of Cuboid**

9cm

### 4) _Pyramid_

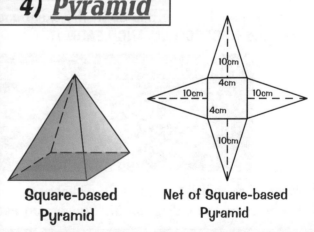

10cm

4cm

10cm     10cm

4cm

10cm

**Square-based Pyramid**

**Net of Square-based Pyramid**

## _The Acid Test:_

LEARN the <u>4 details on surface area and nets</u> and the <u>FOUR NETS</u> on this page, and also the little <u>diagram</u> at the top of the page.

Now cover the page and write down everything you've learnt.
1) Work out the area of all four nets shown above.

# Vectors

<u>4 MONSTROUSLY IMPORTANT THINGS</u> you need to know about <u>*Vectors*</u>:

## 1) *The Four Notations*

The vector shown here can be referred to as

$\begin{pmatrix} 7 \\ 4 \end{pmatrix}$ or <u>a</u> or **a** (in bold type) or $\overrightarrow{AB}$

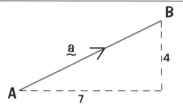

*It's pretty obvious what these mean. Just make sure you know which is which in the column vector ($x \rightarrow$ and $y \uparrow$) and what a negative value means in a column vector.*

## 2) *Adding And Subtracting Vectors*

Vectors must always be added <u>END TO END</u>, so that the <u>arrows all point</u> <u>WITH each other</u>, not AGAINST each other.

*Adding and subtracting*
<u>COLUMN VECTORS</u> *is really easy:* **E.g.** *if* $a = \begin{pmatrix} 5 \\ 3 \end{pmatrix}$ *and* $b = \begin{pmatrix} -2 \\ 4 \end{pmatrix}$ *then* $2a - b = 2\begin{pmatrix} 5 \\ 3 \end{pmatrix} - \begin{pmatrix} -2 \\ 4 \end{pmatrix} = \begin{pmatrix} 12 \\ 2 \end{pmatrix}$

## 3) *Splitting Into Components*

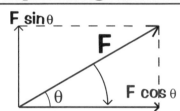

<u>*Any vector can be split into two components*</u> *that are at $90^0$ to each other. These two components will always be* <u>$F\cos\theta$ and $F\sin\theta$</u> *. The main difficulty is knowing which one is which. A <u>very good way to remember it is this</u>:*

When you <u>turn F through angle $\theta$</u> as shown, you get <u>F COS$\theta$</u> (So the <u>other one</u> must be Fsin$\theta$)

## 4) *A Typical Exam Question*

This is a common type of question and it illustrates a very important vector technique:

To obtain the <u>unknown vector</u> just <u>'get there'</u> by any route <u>made up of known vectors</u>

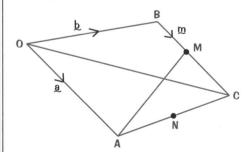

Applying this rule we can easily obtain the following vectors in term of **a**, **b** and **m**, (given that M and N are mid points):

1) $\overrightarrow{AM} = -\underset{\sim}{a} + \underset{\sim}{b} + \underset{\sim}{m}$   (i.e. get there via O and B)

2) $\overrightarrow{OC} = \underset{\sim}{b} + 2\underset{\sim}{m}$   (i.e. get there via B and M)

3) $\overrightarrow{AC} = -\underset{\sim}{a} + \underset{\sim}{b} + 2\underset{\sim}{m}$   (A to C via O, B and M)

## *The Acid Test:*

LEARN the important details on this page, then <u>turn over and write them down</u>.

1) For the diagram above express the following in terms of **a**, **b** and **m**:

   a) $\overrightarrow{MO}$   b) $\overrightarrow{AN}$   c) $\overrightarrow{BN}$   d) $\overrightarrow{NM}$

# "Real life" Vector Questions

These are the types of vector question you're most likely to get in the Exam, so make sure you learn all the little tricks on this page.

## 1) The Old "Swimming Across the River" Question

This is a really easy question: You just _ADD the two velocity vectors END TO END_ and draw the _RESULTANT vector_ which shows both the _speed and direction of the final course_. Simple huh?

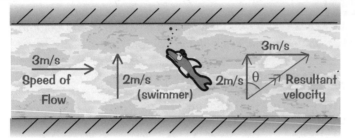

Overall Speed =
$$\sqrt{3^2 + 2^2} = \sqrt{13} = \underline{3.6 \text{m/s}}$$

Direction: TAN θ = 3 ÷ 2
θ = TAN⁻¹ (1.5) = $\underline{56.3^0}$

_As usual with vectors_, you'll need to use _Pythagoras and Trig_ to find the length and angle but that's no big deal is it? Just make sure you **LEARN** the two methods in this question.

The example shown above is absolutely dog-standard stuff and you should definitely see it that way, rather than as one random question of which there may be hundreds — there aren't!

## 2) The Old "Swimming Slightly Upstream" Question

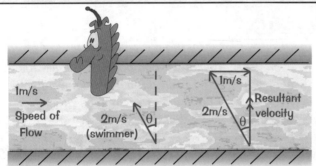

1) SIN θ = OPP/HYP
= 1/2
so θ = SIN⁻¹ (0.5) = $\underline{30^0}$

2) Speed = $\sqrt{2^2 - 1^2} = \sqrt{3} =$
$\underline{1.73 \text{ m/s}}$

The general idea here is to _end up going directly across the river_, and _ONCE AGAIN the old faithful method_ of _DRAWING A VECTOR TRIANGLE_ makes light work of the whole thing — 2 vectors joined _END TO END_ to give the resultant velocity. However, in this case the resultant is drawn in FIRST (straight across), so that _the angle θ has to be worked out to fit_ as shown above.

## 3) The Old "Queen Mary's Tugboats" Question

The problem here is to find the overall force from the two tugs.

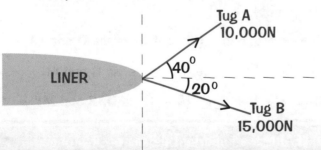

This can be tackled by working out the COMPONENTS of the two force vectors along both dotted lines (F COS θ and F SIN θ etc.)

## The Acid Test:

LEARN the 3 EXAMPLES on this page, then _turn over and write them out_, but with _different numbers_.

1) Work out the overall force on the Queen Mary in example 3.

# Uses of Coordinates

Here's a few more bits and bobs to do with coordinates.

## Use Pythagoras to find the Length of a Line...

**Example:** *"Point P has coordinates (8, 3) and point Q has coordinates (-4, 8). Find the length of the line PQ."*

If you get a question like this, follow these rules and it'll all become breathtakingly simple:

> 1) Draw a *sketch* to find the *right-angled triangle*.
>
> 2) Find the *lengths of the sides* of the triangle.
>
> 3) *Use Pythagoras* to find the *length of the diagonal*. (That's your answer.)

**Solution:**

①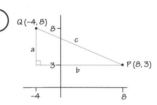

② Length of *side a* = 8 – 3 = 5
Length of *side b* = 8 – -4 = 12

③ *Use Pythagoras* to find *side c*:
$c^2 = a^2 + b^2 = 5^2 + 12^2 = 25 + 144 = 169$
So: $c = \sqrt{169} = 13$

## ... and with a Bit More Fiddling you can find the Midpoint

Same kind of idea — except you don't need Pythagoras this time. Hurrah.

> 1) Find the *average* of the *two x-coordinates*, then do the same for the *y-coordinates*.
> 2) *These will be the coordinates of the midpoint.*

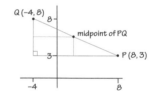

**Example:**

*"Point P has coordinates (8, 3) and point Q has coordinates (-4, 8). Find the midpoint of the line PQ."*

**Solution:**

Average of *x-coordinates* = (8 + -4)/2 = 2
Average of *y-coordinates* = (8 + 3)/2 = 5.5

So, coordinates of midpoint = *(2, 5.5)*

## 3-D Coordinates — easy as XYZ

If the examiners are feeling really mean, they may throw in one of these. So you may as well be prepared.

**3-D COORDINATES ARE ALWAYS WRITTEN (x, y, z) — IN THAT ORDER**

You tip the x-axis and the y-axis over to make the base, and draw the z-axis sticking up out of the origin to make your third dimension.

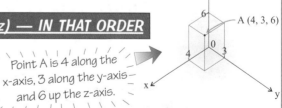

Point A is 4 along the x-axis, 3 along the y-axis and 6 up the z-axis.

## The Acid Test:

LEARN the lists of instructions on this page, then turn over and write them down from memory.

1) Point A has coordinates (10, 15) and point B has coordinates (6, 12). Find the length and midpoint of the line AB.

2) A point is 2 along the x-axis, 1 along the y-axis and 3 up the z-axis. Write its coordinates.

# Loci and Constructions

A <u>LOCUS</u> (another ridiculous maths word) is simply:

## A LINE that shows <u>all the points which fit in with a given rule</u>

Make sure you <u>learn</u> how to do these <u>PROPERLY</u> using a <u>RULER AND COMPASSES</u>.

## 1) The locus of points which are <u>"A FIXED DISTANCE from a given POINT"</u>

This locus is simply a <u>CIRCLE</u>.

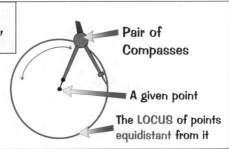

Pair of Compasses

A given point

The LOCUS of points equidistant from it

## 2) The locus of points which are <u>"A FIXED DISTANCE from a given LINE"</u>

This locus is an <u>OVAL SHAPE</u>

It has <u>straight sides</u> (drawn with a <u>ruler</u>) and <u>ends</u> which are <u>perfect semicircles</u> (drawn with <u>compasses</u>).

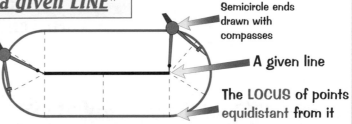

Semicircle ends drawn with compasses

A given line

The LOCUS of points equidistant from it

## 3) The locus of points which are <u>"EQUIDISTANT from TWO GIVEN LINES"</u>

1) Keep the compass setting <u>THE SAME</u> while you make <u>all four marks</u>.

2) Make sure you <u>leave</u> your compass marks <u>showing</u>.

3) You get <u>two equal angles</u> — i.e. this <u>LOCUS</u> is actually an <u>ANGLE BISECTOR</u>.

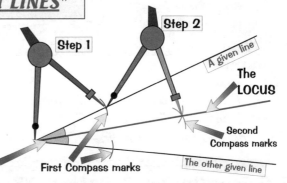

Step 1
Step 2
A given line
The LOCUS
Second Compass marks
The other given line
First Compass marks

## 4) The locus of points which are <u>"EQUIDISTANT from TWO GIVEN POINTS"</u>

(In the diagram below, A and B are the two given points)

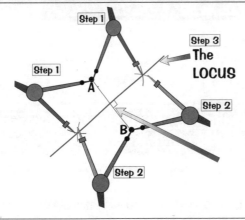

Step 1
Step 3
The LOCUS
Step 1
Step 2
Step 2
A
B

<u>This LOCUS</u> is all the points which are the <u>same distance</u> from A and B.

This time the locus is actually the <u>PERPENDICULAR BISECTOR</u> of the line joining the two points.

# Loci and Constructions

## Constructing accurate 60° angles

1) They may well ask you to draw an *accurate 60° angle*.

2) One place they're needed is for drawing an *equilateral triangle*.

3) Make sure you *follow the method* shown in this diagram, and that you can do it *entirely from memory*.

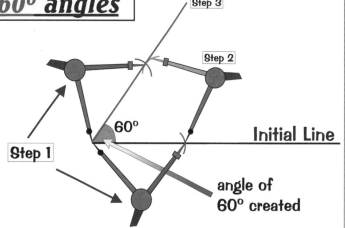

Step 3

Step 2

Step 1

60°

Initial Line

angle of 60° created

## Constructing accurate 90° angles

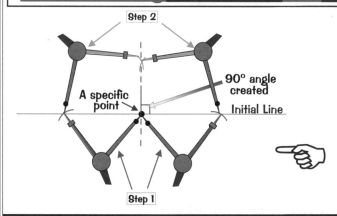

Step 2

90° angle created

A specific point

Initial Line

Step 1

1) They might want you to draw an *accurate 90° angle*.

2) They won't accept it just done "*by eye*" or with a ruler — if you want the marks you've got to do it *the proper way* with *compasses* like I've shown you here.

3) Make sure you can *follow the method* shown in this diagram.

## Drawing the Perpendicular from a Point to a Line

1) This is similar to the one above but *not quite the same* — make sure you can do *both*.

2) Again, they won't accept it just done "*by eye*" or with a ruler — you've got to do it *the proper way* with *compasses*.

3) *Learn* the diagram.

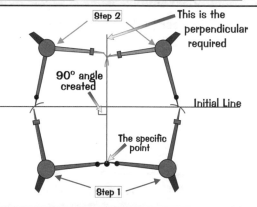

Step 2

This is the perpendicular required

90° angle created

Initial Line

The specific point

Step 1

## The Acid Test: LEARN EVERYTHING ON THESE TWO PAGES

Now cover up these two pages and draw an example of each of the four loci.
Also draw an equilateral triangle and a square, both with fabulously accurate 60° and 90° angles.
Also, draw a line and a point and construct the perpendicular from the point to the line.

# Time Series

## Time Series — Measure the Same Thing over a Period of Time

A time series is what you get if you measure the
same thing at a number of different times.

**EXAMPLE:** Measuring the temperature in your greenhouse
at 12 o'clock each day gives you a time series — other
examples might be profit figures, crime figures or rainfall.

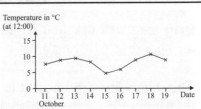

*THE RETAIL PRICE INDEX (RPI) IS A TIME SERIES:* *Every month, the prices of loads of items (same ones
each month) — are combined to get an index number called the RPI, which is a kind of average.
As goods get more expensive, this index number gets higher and higher. So when you see on TV that inflation this
month is 2.5%, what it actually means is that the RPI is increasing at an annual rate of 2.5%.*

## Seasonality — The Same Basic Pattern

This is when there's a definite pattern that **REPEATS ITSELF** every so often.
This is called **SEASONALITY** and the "*so often*" is called the **PERIOD**.

To find the **PERIOD**, measure **PEAK TO PEAK** (or trough to trough).

This series has a *period of 12 months*. There are a few irregularities,
so the pattern isn't exactly the same every 12 months, but it's about right.

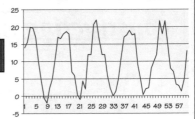

## Trend — Ignoring the Wrinkles

This time series has lots of random fluctuations
but there's a definite upwards *trend*.

The pink line is the trend line.
It's straight, so this is a *linear* trend.

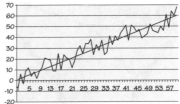

## Moving Average — Smooths Out the Seasonality

It's easier to spot a trend if you can 'get rid of' the seasonality and some of the irregularities.
One way to smooth the series is to use a *moving average*.

This is a time series that definitely looks
periodic — but it's
difficult to tell if
there's a trend.

The period is 12, so you
use 12 values for the
moving average:

*... but plot the
moving average*
(in pink — must be pink —
that's dead important)...

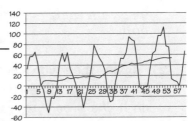

...and you can easily see the *upward
trend*.

**HOW TO FIND A MOVING AVERAGE:**

Find the average of
these 12 values...

...then of these...

...then of these,
and so on.

| month | 1 | 2 | 3 | 4 | 5 | 6 | 7 | 8 | 9 | 10 | 11 | 12 | 13 | 14 | ... |
|---|---|---|---|---|---|---|---|---|---|---|---|---|---|---|---|
| temperature | 38.00 | 42.30 | 59.00 | 32.30 | 25.00 | 2.00 | -5.00 | -51.30 | -35.00 | -45.30 | -22.00 | 1.00 | 49.00 | 62.30 | ... |

## The Acid Test: LEARN the words TIME SERIES, SEASONALITY, PERIOD, TREND, MOVING AVERAGE. Cover the page and write a description of each.

1) My town's rainfall is measured every month for 20 yrs and graphed. There's a rough pattern, which repeats
itself every 4 months. a) What is the period of this time series? b) Describe how to calculate a moving average.

# Probability — Tree Diagrams

## General Tree Diagram

Tree Diagrams are all pretty much the same, so it's a pretty darned good idea to learn these basic details (which apply to <u>ALL</u> tree diagrams) — ready for the one in the Exam.

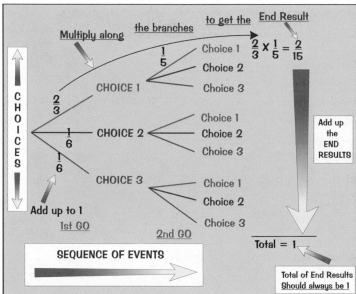

1) Always <u>**MULTIPLY ALONG THE BRANCHES**</u> (as shown) to get the END RESULTS.

2) <u>*On any set of branches which all meet at a point*</u>, the numbers must always <u>ADD UP TO 1</u>.

3) <u>*Check that your diagram is correct*</u> by <u>making sure the End Results ADD UP TO ONE</u>.

4) <u>*To answer any question*</u>, simply <u>ADD UP THE RELEVANT END RESULTS</u> (see below).

## A likely Tree Diagram Question

<u>EXAMPLE</u>: *"A box contains 5 red disks and 3 green disks. Two disks are taken <u>without replacement</u>. Draw a tree diagram and hence find the probability that both disks are the same colour."*

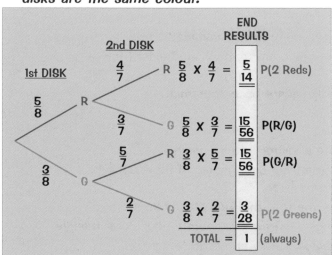

<u>*Once the tree diagram is drawn*</u> all you then need to do to answer the question is simply <u>select the RELEVANT END RESULTS</u> and then <u>ADD THEM TOGETHER</u>:

2 REDS    (5/14)
2 GREENS    (3/28)

$$\frac{5}{14} + \frac{3}{28} = \frac{13}{28}$$

If you can, use a calculator for this. Otherwise, use the fraction rules on P.10.

## The Acid Test:

LEARN the <u>GENERAL DIAGRAM</u> for Tree Diagrams and the <u>4 points</u> that go with them.

1) O.K. let's see what you've learnt shall we:
   *TURN OVER AND WRITE DOWN EVERYTHING YOU KNOW ABOUT TREE DIAGRAMS.*

2) A bag contains 6 red tarantulas and 4 black tarantulas. If two girls each pluck out a tarantula at random without replacement, draw a tree diagram to find the probability that they get different coloured ones.

# Revision Test for Stage Three

Here's the really fun page. The inevitable list of straight-down-the-middle questions to test how much you know. Remember, these questions will sort out quicker than anything else can, exactly what you _know_ and what you _don't_. And that's exactly what revision is all about, don't forget: finding out what you DON'T know and then learning it until you do. Enjoy.

## Keep learning these basic facts until you know them

1) Write out the eight rules for dealing with powers.
2) Give the formula for compound growth and decay, and explain what each term means.
3) Name three different forms that a rational number can take, and give an example for each.
4) What is an irrational number? Give two examples.
5) What is a surd? Write down all you know about manipulating surds.
6) What does D.O.T.S. stand for? Give two examples of it.
7) What are simultaneous equations? List the 6 steps of the method for solving them.
8) Describe the method for solving simultaneous equations with graphs.
9) Describe the method for solving a quadratic equation by factorising.
10) Write down the general equation for a straight line.
11) How can you find the solutions to a quadratic equation from its graph?
12) Sketch the graphs for $y=x^3$ and $y=1/x$.
13) List 5 rules of circle geometry.

14) For this shape, draw: a) the front elevation, b) the side elevation, c) the plan

15) Define the terms "congruent" and "similar".
16) Explain how to identify a formula as a length, an area or a volume?
17) Write down the conversion factors between $mm^3$, $cm^3$ and $m^3$ in standard form.
18) Sketch the nets for these shapes:
    a) triangular prism, b) cube, c) cuboid, d) square-based pyramid.
19) What are the four vector notations?
20) Draw diagrams to show:
    a) adding two vectors together, b) splitting a vector into its components.
21) Describe how to find the length of a line, given the coordinates of its endpoints. Describe how to find the midpoint of the same line.
22) What is a locus? Describe, with diagrams, the four that you should know.
23) Demonstrate how to draw accurate 60° angles. Draw an accurate equilateral triangle.
24) Demonstrate how to draw accurate 90° angles. Draw an accurate square.
25) Which one of these is NOT a time series?
    a) measuring the temperature in 20 different countries at 12:00 today, GMT,
    b) measuring the temperature in Britain at 12:00 every day for 100 days,
    c) the Retail Price Index.
26) How can you find out if a seasonal time series has an overall trend?
27) Draw a general tree diagram and label it fully.

# Answers

## Stage One — Acid Tests

P.1 <u>BIG NUMBERS & ROUNDING</u>: <u>1)</u> 0.008, 0.09, 0.1, 0.2, 0.307, 0.37   <u>2a)</u> 450 <u>b)</u> 680 <u>c)</u> 50 <u>d)</u> 10

P.2 <u>NEGATIVE NUMBERS</u>: <u>1)</u> -23,-22,-12,-5,-1,0,4,7,10,45   <u>2)</u> 21°C   <u>3a)</u> –15  <u>b)</u> 5

P.3 <u>PRIME NUMBERS</u>: <u>1)</u> 2,3,5,7,11,13,17,19,23,29,31,37,41,43,47   <u>2)</u> 97, 101, 103, 107, 109

P.4 <u>MULTIPLES, FACTORS AND PRIME FACTORS</u>: <u>1)</u> 7,14,21,28,35,42,49,56,63,70 and 9,18,27,36,
45,54,63,72,81,90  <u>2)</u> 1,2,3,4,6,9,12,18,36 and 1,2,3,4,6,7,12,14,21,28,42,84  <u>3a)</u> 2×3×3×5×11 <u>b)</u>
2×2×2×2×2×5   P.5 <u>LCM AND HCF</u>: <u>1)</u> 8,16,24,32,40,48,56,64,72,80 and 9,18,27,36,45,54,63,72,81,90
LCM = 72  <u>2)</u> 1,2,4,7,8,14,28,56 and 1,2,4,8,13,26,52,104 HCF = 8  <u>3)</u> 63  <u>4)</u> 12

P.6 <u>SPECIAL NUMBER SEQUENCES</u>: <u>1)</u> EVENS: 2,4,6,8,10,12,14,16,18,20,22,24,26,28,30;
ODDS: 1,3,5,7,9,11,13,15,17,19,21,23,25,27,29; SQUARES:1,4,9,16,25,36,49,64,81,100,121,144,169,196,225;
CUBES: 1,8,27,64,125,216,343,512,729,1000,1331,1728,2197,2744,3375; POWERS OF 2: 2,4,8,16,32,64,
128,256,512,1024,2048,4096,8192,16384,32768; POWERS OF 10: 10, 100, 1000, 10 000, 100 000,
1 000 000, 10 000 000, 100 000 000, 1 000 000 000, 10 000 000 000, 100 000 000 000, 1 000 000 000 000,
10 000 000 000 000, 100 000 000 000 000, 1 000 000 000 000 000 hmm...; TRIANGLE Nos: 1,3,6,10,15,21,
28,36,45,55,66,78,91,105,120  <u>2a)</u> 56, 134, 156, 36, 64 <u>b)</u> 23, 45, 81, 25, 97, 125, 1 <u>c)</u> 81, 25, 36, 1, 64
<u>d)</u> 125, 1, 64  <u>e)</u> 64  <u>f)</u> 45, 36, 1       P.7 <u>SQUARE ROOTS AND CUBE ROOTS</u>:<u>1a)</u>  7.48 and -7.48
<u>b)</u> 7.66 <u>c)</u> 14.14 and -14.14  <u>d)</u> 20   <u>2a)</u> 6 or -6  <u>b)</u> 4  <u>c)</u> 3 or -3

P.8 <u>MULTIPLYING & DIVIDING BY 10, 100..</u>: <u>1)</u> <u>a)</u> 345  <u>b)</u> 9650  <u>c)</u> 960   <u>2a)</u> 6.542  <u>b)</u> 0.00308  <u>c)</u> 12

P.9 <u>FRACTIONS, DECIMALS AND PERCENTAGES</u>:

P.11 <u>FRACTIONS</u>: <u>1a)</u> 3/8  <u>b)</u> 2 $^7/_{10}$  <u>c)</u> 11/15   <u>d)</u> x = 13
<u>e)</u> y = 1  <u>f)</u> 0.375  <u>g)</u> 35/1000 = 7/200   <u>2a)</u> 8/15
<u>b)</u> 8/3 = 2 $^2/_3$  <u>c)</u> 1/2   <u>d)</u> 3/7  <u>e)</u> 84   <u>f)</u> 84 $^{12}/_{19}$

P.12 <u>PERCENTAGES</u>: <u>1)</u> 40%   <u>2)</u> £20,500   <u>3)</u> 1.39%

P.15 <u>FORMULAS FROM WORDS</u>: <u>1)</u> Y = 5X – 3   <u>2)</u> C = 95n

P.16 <u>SUBSTITUTING VALUES INTO FORMULAS</u>: <u>2)</u> 25

| Fraction | Decimal | Percentage |
|----------|---------|------------|
| 1/5 | 0.2 | 20% |
| 7/20 | 0.35 | 35% |
| 9/20 | 0.45 | 45% |
| 3/25 | 0.12 | 12% |
| 1/8 | 0.125 | 12.5% |
| 77/100 | 0.77 | 77% |

P.18 <u>BASIC ALGEBRA</u>: <u>1a)</u> $4x + y – 4$ <u>b)</u> $4y^2 – 2k + 2$ <u>c)</u> $2x + 2$   <u>2a)</u> $6p^2q – 8pq^3$ <u>b)</u> $8g^2 + 16g – 10$
<u>c)</u> $16 – 24h + 9h^2$   <u>3a)</u> $7xy^2(2xy + 3 – 5x^2y^2)$ <u>b)</u> $6h^2j(2j^2 + h^2jk – 6hk)$

P.20 <u>SOLVING EQUATIONS</u>: <u>1)</u> x = 8   <u>2)</u> x = 7   P.21 <u>SOLVING EQUATIONS</u>: <u>1)</u> x = 2   <u>2)</u> x = $-^1/_5$

P.22 <u>NUMBER PATTERNS</u>: <u>2a)</u> 162, 486  <u>b)</u> 18, 29  <u>c)</u> 23, 30   <u>d)</u> 16, 8

P.23 <u>FINDING THE N<sup>TH</sup> TERM</u>: <u>1a)</u> 3n + 1  <u>b)</u> 5n – 2  <u>c)</u> ½n(n + 1)   <u>d)</u> $n^2 – 2n + 4$

P.24 <u>COORDINATES</u>: <u>1)</u> A(4,5)   B(6,0)   C(5,-5)   D(0,-3)   E(-5,-2)   F(-4,0)   G(-3,3)   H(0,5)   <u>2)</u> Rhombus

P.25  <u>REGULAR POLYGONS</u>: <u>5)</u> Ext. ang. = 72°, Int. ang. = 108°  <u>6)</u> Ext. ang. = 30°, Int. ang. = 150°

P.27  <u>TRANSFORMATIONS</u>: A→B,   Rotation of 90° clockwise about the origin.   B→C,   Reflection in the
line Y = X.       C→A, Reflection in the Y-axis.       A→D, Translation of [-9, -7]

P.28  <u>COMBINATIONS OF TRANSFORMATIONS</u>: <u>1)</u> e.g. C→D Rotation 90° anti-clockwise about
the origin, translation of [0, 3].   D→C Rotation 270° anti-clockwise about the origin,
translation of [-3, 0].   <u>2)</u> A'→B Rotation 180° about the point (0, 3).

P.30 <u>CIRCLES</u>: <u>1)</u> C = 44.0 cm

P.32 <u>GEOMETRY</u>: <u>1)</u>  z = 65°   <u>2)</u> 360°   <u>3)</u> 540°     <u>4)</u> 120° and 60° all round

P.33 <u>BEARINGS</u>: <u>1)</u> 118°   <u>2)</u> 298°

P.34 <u>CONVERSION FACTORS</u>: <u>1)</u> 2,300m   <u>2)</u> £34   <u>3)</u> 3.2cm

P.39 <u>PROBABILITY</u>: <u>1)</u> $^4/_7$, 0   <u>2)</u> 0.78   <u>3)</u> H-1, H-2, H-3, H-4, H-5, H-6, T-1, T-2, T-3, T-4, T-5, T-6

## Revision Test for Stage One

<u>18)</u> C= nX + mY  <u>19)</u> C = (4 × 26) + (7 × 18) = 230   <u>21)</u> $4xy^3(3x^2y + xz – 2)$   <u>36)</u> all values of x from 50
to 60, including 50 but excluding 60.  <u>38)</u> 1 – x

## Stage Two — Acid Tests

P.41 <u>ROUNDING OFF</u>: <u>1)</u> 3.57   <u>2)</u> 0.05   <u>3)</u> 12.910   <u>4)</u> 3546.1   <u>5a)</u> 568 (rule 3)      <u>b)</u> 23400 (rule 3)
<u>c)</u> 0.0456 (rules 1 and 3)     <u>d)</u> 0.909 (rules 1, 2 and 3)

P.44 <u>STANDARD INDEX FORM</u>: <u>2)</u> $9.58 × 10^5$   <u>3)</u> $1.8 × 10^{-4}$   <u>4)</u> 4560   <u>5)</u> $2 × 10^{21}$ , 2,000,00.....(21 zeros!)

P.46 <u>RATIOS</u>: <u>1a)</u> 5:7   <u>b)</u> 2:3   <u>c)</u> 3:5   <u>2)</u> 17.5 bowls   <u>3)</u> £3500:£2100:£2800

P.47 <u>REARRANGING FORMULAS</u>: <u>1)</u> C $=\frac{5}{9}$ (F – 32)   <u>2)</u> a) p = -4y/3  b) p = $\sqrt{\dfrac{y}{x^2 – 3}}$

P.48 <u>INEQUALITIES</u>: <u>1)</u> X ⩾ -2   <u>2)</u> -4, -3, -2 , -1, 0, 1      P.49 <u>TRIAL AND IMPROVEMENT</u>: <u>1)</u> X = 1.6

# Answers

## Stage Two — Acid Tests (continued)

P.50 <u>FINDING THE GRADIENT OF A LINE</u>: 1) gradient = -1½

P.51 <u>PLOTTING STRAIGHT LINE GRAPHS</u>: 1)

P.54 <u>TYPICAL GRAPH QUESTIONS</u>:

1)

| x | -2 | -1 | 0 | 1 | 2 | 3 | 4 | 5 | 6 |
|---|----|----|---|---|---|---|---|---|---|
| y | 15 | 8 | 3 | 0 | -1 | 0 | 3 | 8 | 15 |

2) Y = 3.8,  X = -1.6 and 5.6     3) Miles per gallon, i.e. fuel consumption

P.55 <u>PYTHAGORAS' THEOREM</u>: 1) BC = 8m     2) Yes, because $a^2 + b^2 = h^2$ works.

P.57 <u>TRIGONOMETRY</u>: 1) X = 26.5m     2) 23.6°     3) 32.6° (both)

P.60 <u>DENSITY & SPEED</u>: 2) 16.5 g/cm³     3) 603g     5) Time = 7½ hrs   Dist = 11.2km

P.62 <u>VOLUME OR CAPACITY</u>: a) Trapezoidal Prism, V = 148.5 cm³     b) Cylinder, V = 0.70 m³

P.63 <u>PIE CHARTS</u>:

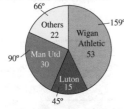

P.65 <u>MEAN, MEDIAN, MODE & RANGE</u>:

First, do this:   -14, -12, -5, -5, 0, 1, 3, 6, 7, 8, 10, 14, 18, 23, 25

Mean = 5.27,  Median = 6,   Mode = -5,  Range = 39

P.66 <u>FREQUENCY TABLES</u>:

| No. of Phones | 0 | 1 | 2 | 3 | 4 | 5 | 6 | TOTALS |
|---|---|---|---|---|---|---|---|---|
| Frequency | 1 | 25 | 53 | 34 | 22 | 5 | 1 | 141 |
| No. × Frequency | 0 | 25 | 106 | 102 | 88 | 25 | 6 | 352 |

Mean = 2.5, Median = 2, Mode = 2, Range = 6

P.67 <u>GROUPED FREQUENCY TABLES</u>:

| Length(cm) | 15.5 — | 16.5 — | 17.5 — | 18.5 — 19.5 | TOTALS |
|---|---|---|---|---|---|
| Frequency | 12 | 18 | 23 | 8 | 61 |
| Mid-Interval Value | 16 | 17 | 18 | 19 | — |
| Freq × M I V | 192 | 306 | 414 | 152 | 1064 |

Mean = 17.4,  Modal Group = 17.5 — 18.5, Median ≈ 17.5

P.68 & 69 <u>CUMULATIVE FREQUENCY</u>:

| Weight (kg) | 41 – 45 | 46 – 50 | 51 – 55 | 56 – 60 | 61 – 65 | 66 – 70 | 71 – 75 |
|---|---|---|---|---|---|---|---|
| Frequency | 2 | 7 | 17 | 25 | 19 | 8 | 2 |
| Cum. Freq. | 2 | 9 | 26 | 51 | 70 | 78 | 80 |

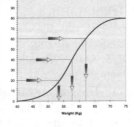

Median = 58 kg, Lower Quartile = 53 kg Upper Quartile = 63 kg Inter-quartile range 10 kg

## Stage Three — Acid Tests

P.71 <u>POWERS</u>: 1a) $3^8$  b) 4  c) $8^{12}$  d) 1  e) $7^6$     2a) $5^{12}$  b) 36 or $6^2$  c) $2^{-3}$

P.72 <u>COMPOUND GROWTH & DECAY</u>: 1) 48 stick insects.   2) 0.15 m/s.

P.73 <u>IRRATIONAL NUMBERS, SURDS & D.O.T.S.</u>: 1a) $4\sqrt{2}$    b) $2+2\sqrt{2}$    2a) $\left(2s^2 + 3t\right)\left(2s^2 - 3t\right)$

b) $2(p+4qr)(p-4qr)$          P.74 <u>SIMULTANEOUS EQUATIONS</u>: F = 3   G = -1

P.75 <u>SIMULTANEOUS EQUATIONS WITH GRAPHS</u>: 2) a) x=2, y=4   b) x=1½, y=3

P.76 <u>QUADRATICS</u>: 1a) x = -2 or -3   b) x = -6 or -2   c) x = 3 or -8   d) x = 7 or -1

P.80 <u>PROJECTIONS, CONGRUENCE & SIMILARITY</u>: 2a) i, ii and iv.     b) i and ii.

P.81 <u>LENGTH, AREA & VOLUME</u>: 1) $\pi r^2$ = area,   Lwh = volume,   $\pi d$ = perimeter,   ½bh = area, 2bh + 4lp = area, $4r^2p + 3\pi d^3$ = volume, 2πr(3L + 5T) = area   2) $6.5 \times 10^{-3}$ m³,   $7.68 \times 10^{-5}$ m³

P.82 <u>SOLIDS AND NETS</u>: 1) 128.8cm²  2) 294cm²  3) 174cm²  4) 96cm²

P.83 <u>VECTORS</u>: 1) a) – m – b    b) ½b – ½a + m (=½$\overrightarrow{AC}$)   c) ½(a – b) + m   d) ½(b – a)

P.84 <u>"REAL LIFE" VECTORS</u>: 1) 21,800N, 3.4° up from the horizontal.

P.85 <u>USES OF COORDINATES</u>: 1) AB = 5; midpoint at (8, 13.5)   2) (2, 1, 3)

P.88 <u>TIME SERIES</u>: 1a) 4 months     P.89 <u>PROBABILITY — TREE DIAGRAMS</u>: 2) P = 8/15

# _Index_

# Index

MEIR41